PROOF THROUGH THE NIGHT

PROOF THROUGH

THE NIGHT

A B-29 Pilot Captive in Japan

The Ernest Pickett Story

as told to K.P. Burke

Opal Creek
Press

To Dave, my buddy. With lots and lots of love. Knish. KP Burke

Opal Creek Press, LLC
Salem, Oregon 97302
Ph: 503-375-9015
www.opalcreekpress.com

All photographs, unless otherwise noted are the property of the author.

The following excerpts are printed with permission or credited as follows:
Those Who Fall, by John Muirhead. Published by Rrandom House, Inc.
So Long Until Tomorrow: From Quaker Hill to Kathmandu, by Lowell Thomas. Copyright © 1977 Lowell Thomas. Reprinted with persmission of Lowell Thomas Jr.
All Quiet On The Western Front by permission of the estate of Paulette G. Remarque.
Excerpt from *Mainichi Shimbun* by permission of Mainichi Shimbun, Tokyo, Japan.
The excerpt from TIME magazine: ©1945 Time Inc.
Crossing Unmarked Snow, William Stafford, University of Michigan Press, 1998.
"The Loud Hour" from *Collected and New Poems 1924-1963* by Mark Van Doren. Copyright ©1963 by Mark Van Doren. Copyright renewed ©1991 by Dorothy G. Van Doren. Reprinted by permission of Hill and Wang, a division of Farrar, Straus and Giroux, LLC.

Printed on acid free recycled paper.
Manufactured in the United States of America.
Opal Creek Press and the Opal Creek Press logo are trademarks belonging to Opal Creek Press, LLC.

Library of Congress Cataloging-in-Publication Data
Pickett, Ernest, 1918-1999.
Proof through the night : a B-29 pilot captive in Japan : the Ernest Pickett story / as told to K. P. Burke.
    p. cm.
Includes index.
ISBN 1-931105-04-9 (alk. paper)
1. Pickett, Ernest, 1918-1999. 2. World War, 1939-1945--Personal narratives, American. 3. Bomber pilots-United States-Biography. 4. B-29 bomber. 5. World War, 1939-1945--Aerial operations, American. 6. World War, 1939-1945--Prisoners and prisons, Japanese. 7. Prisoners of war-Japan-Biography. 8. Prisoners of war-United States-Biography.
I. Burke, K. P., 1956- II. Title.
D811.P51656 A3 2001
940.54'7252'092--dc21

2001004846

To Faye, of course,
and to the crew of the Reddy Teddy,
the men of the 468th Bomb Group
and all those who gave so much.

Table of Contents

List of Illustrations

Foreword

By Lt. Gen. James V. Edmundson, USAF, retired

Over his 36-year military career, James Edmundson repeatedly demonstrated his exceptional leadership ability. He flew over ten thousand hours in 137 different types of airplanes, including 181 combat missions in three wars. Some of the posts he held include Director of Operations at the Strategic Air Command, Commander of the 17th Air Force, which included all of the American fighter units committed to NATO, Vice Commander-in-Chief of the Pacific Air Force during the Vietnam War, Deputy Commander-in-Chief of Strike Command, and two posts at the Pentagon. He retired as a three star Lieutenant General.

His posts and rankings, however, were only part of his achievement. He was a most beloved and respected officer. The inner strength, courage, integrity, humanity, and warmth that he exhibited as a squadron commander in the Army Air Corps' fledgling 20th Air Force typified him throughout his career. Men who served with him in those early B-29 days still hold him in the highest regard, and refer to him affectionately as Colonel Jim. Others who met him later, with the same affection, address him as General Jim.

This is the story of a brave and capable young American named Ernest A. Pickett. His is a fascinating story and one that needs telling. He participated in events that haven't found their way into most of our history books and are at risk of falling through history's cracks. For example, most people living today associate the B-29 in World War II in terms of operations based in the Pacific and the dropping of the atomic bomb. They have never heard of the massive undertaking of operating B-29s from India and China before the Pacific bases were possible. They have never heard of the daring missions over the Himalayas that cost so many American lives.

Ernie's account of being shot down over the steel mills of Yawata on the Japanese home island of Kyushu and the inhumane treatment of POWs in Japanese prisons and camps is also important history. These stories must be told and have been largely overlooked. Without them, we cannot have a complete picture of the war with Japan.

As Ernie tells his personal story, he also tells the story of the early B-29. He tells how it felt to be a young pilot taking part in establishing the 58th Wing, the first of the B-29 outfits. The B-29 was developed under tremendous pressure during time of war and was a remarkable plane. As Ernie shows us, there weren't enough B-29s available for training in those early days in Kansas. Much of the training time we had was spent working out the kinks in the new planes. The 58th Wing consisted of four groups. Each of those had four squadrons of fifteen crews. When the 58th Wing shook off the Kansas dust and headed off for war, the 240 aircraft commanders who flew the planes averaged less than fifty hours of B-29 flying time.

Because the Army knew there would be little actual flying time available for those first crews, the very wise decision had been made in Washington to man the 58th Wing with hand-picked men. As much combat experience as possible was fed into the outfits. Returnees from the Philippines, the South Pacific and North Africa were brought into the wing. All four group commanders and eight of the sixteen squadron commanders were going out on their second combat tour. A smattering of combat experience was sprinkled throughout the groups, but the vast majority of personnel came hand-picked from the cream of the stateside outfits and the training pipeline. Ernie Pickett didn't know it at the time, but his winding up in the 792nd squadron of the 468th Group of the 58th Wing was no accident. He had been specifically selected for the job.

When the 58th Wing arrived in the China-Burma-India (CBI) Theater in the Spring of 1944, its published mission was to carry the war to the Japanese, both to their home islands and to the far reaches of eastern Asia, which were being held in bondage by the Japanese armed forces. The B-29s of the 58th Wing hit targets as far north as the steel mills of Mukden in Manchuria and as far south as the oil refineries of Palembang in Sumatra. They supported General MacArthur's return to the Phillippines by hitting airfields in Taiwan. The key strike missions, however, were against the industrial complexes on the home islands of Japan which, except for the Doolittle raid, had not been touched by U.S. airpower.

The second, and equally important mission of the 58th Wing was the developmental testing of every B-29 it received. We were taking an untested plane to combat in the world's most demanding climate and over the world's most inhospitable terrain. The B-29's Wright R3350 engines were brand new. Many of the modifications that eventually gave it reliability were developed in India and China as the 58th Wing flew fuel and bombs across the Himalayas, known familiarly as "The Hump," to support its operations out of China. Short cowl flaps to permit increased engine cooling with less drag, crossover tubes to provide better lubrication to the top cylinders, and cast iron valve guides to replace the bronze ones with which it was initially equipped, were three engine modifications developed in the CBI.

Modifications to the airplane itself originating in the CBI also helped give the B-29 the effectiveness and reliability it had later in the war. The center wing fuel tanks increased range, the four-gun upper-forward turret provided better protective fire, and the pop-open bomb bay doors added greater tactical flexibility in the target area.

When, in May 1945, the 58th Wing moved to West Field Tinian, it joined the three wings that were established in the Marianas, later to be joined by the 315th Wing, and became part of the most awesome collection of strategic air power ever assembled. Raids against the Japanese Empire by one thousand B-29s became regular and frequent.

Looking up from his prisoner-of-war compound, Ernie Pickett watched the culmination of the B-29 campaign he had helped to pioneer. He had participated in the development of the plane that would bring the Japanese Empire to its knees, thus making unnecessary the amphibious beachhead landings on Japanese shores that would have cost millions of lives in a Japanese D-Day and ensuing campaign.

It's important for Americans of this day to know and understand the patriotism and courage of the men of Ernie's generation and of the women who stood behind them. The freedom we enjoy was largely purchased by the sacrifices of Ernie Pickett and millions of men like him who, with dignity, honor, and pride, did what had to be done, because there was nobody else to do it.

Ernie's story will hold your attention, as it did mine, and it will give you a sense of pride to hear from one of the generation of young Americans who never hesitated to lay it all on the line when their country needed them.

To Fly

"The sky filled our senses beyond anything we had ever come upon. In that blue crucible our youth had at last reached the place to spend itself."

John Muirhead
Those Who Fall

"How did I end up here?" Haven't we all asked ourselves that question at some point in our lives? There's that feeling of unreality, a sense of trying to grasp a situation we never anticipated. I certainly had that feeling as I fell toward Earth the day I parachuted out of my plane over Japan. One minute I was flying what felt like an invincible war machine, the next minute I was out in the atmosphere, miles above the ground, alone. My training kicked in and got my parachute open at the right time, but it couldn't solve the other problem I could see rising toward me. There was no way around it. I was about to die.

My older brother, Gene, bought me my first airplane ride when I was seventeen and a senior in high school. It was 1936 and we belonged to a group of friends who had grown up in the woods of Oregon, in Azalea, a wide spot in the road my grandfather had named. The Depression had hit us hard, and as boys we all had gone barefoot whenever possible to save our only pair of shoes, and belonged to families always needing the next dollar. The oldest boys in the group, having graduated from high school and now earning

1

men's wages in the woods or area mills, had discovered that without families to feed or homes to support, they could help their parents financially and still have plenty of cash in their pockets.

Typical of boys in every generation since, there was only one logical thing these young men could see to do with all that extra money. They bought cars. Three of the group, including my brother, had cars, and with money jangling in their pockets, their girlfriends beside them and we younger boys in tow, they gassed up the "whoopies" and headed to Crescent City, California. The beach.

As the winding road led us from thick forests of familiar Douglas Fir into groves of gigantic Coastal Redwood, we basked in the freedom the first road trip of youth universally symbolizes. Laughing and playful, and probably driving too fast, we reveled in our independence and maturity.

In those days, you could take your cars on the beach and we sped up and down the sand, cutting cookies and playing. Our friend, Orval, a tall curly-headed blond, provided the inevitable disaster when he locked up the transmission on his brand new Chevrolet driving too fast in reverse.

But with all the youthful skylarking, the trip provided one profound experience for me. For there, parked on the sand at Crescent City, was a gleaming yellow biplane. The pilot, using the beaches up and down the coast as airstrips, was selling rides and Gene bought one for me.

I remember squeezing into the front seat with another kid, Glen Kafer, and adjusting my goggles, thrilling to the vibrations that shivered through the plane as the pilot revved the engine.

"You want a fun ride?" the pilot shouted as we prepared for takeoff. "Of course," we nodded.

Soaring above the blue Pacific that day in that loud, windy biplane and seeing the rugged coastline from the air filled my senses beyond anything I had ever imagined. But when the pilot climbed steeply into a loop and brought us swooping out of it, my conversion was complete. Every nerve in my body was tingling and I knew I wanted more.

Having grown up in the age of Lindbergh and barnstormers, I had been intrigued, as were most boys my age, by the idea of flying. But after that ride, flying became my fantasy. From then on, the sound of a plane was like an irresistible summons. I would drop whatever I was doing and hungrily watch any plane that flew over until it was out of sight and gone. I dreamed of being a pilot.

Of course, to a barefoot boy in the woods of Oregon, there was little hope of reaching such a goal. My family was markedly poor in an era of poverty. We had milk for cereal, but never enough to drink, and two changes of clothes, one for school and one for the rest of the time. Because there was no electricity or running water, our after-school chores included keeping enough wood split and stacked for the cooking stove and the fireplace, as well as bringing in water from the pump in back. College was out of the question. We seemed destined to spend our lives in the woods, logging or milling as our father and grandfather had done, becoming bent and hardened at a young age.

And then came a war to break the old patterns and set millions of people spinning in unexpected directions. As the conflict in Europe heated up, American men of draft age were instructed to either enlist or to take a job in the defense industry. Both commitments were for one year. By that time, my family had moved to Sweet Home, Oregon, which was located midway up the Willamette Valley and nestled in the foothills of the Cascades. I was out of school and working in the woods. The War Department had set up a welding school in nearby Lebanon. Working as a welder sounded a lot better than being in the Army, so I paid the tuition, learned to weld, and went to work at the St. Johns shipyards near Portland.

The work at the shipyards was hard. We often had to crawl far into the cramped area between the inner and outer hulls of the ships to weld. We welded in tight, awkward positions, uncomfortably close to our work. The clanging of steel against steel and the pounding of hammers on metal created a constant clamor which was punctuated by the rat-tat-tat of air-powered chippers that worked directly above our heads. The noise was deafening.

In those days, before workman's safety laws, we were exposed to a number of health hazards. Not only did we lack earplugs, but there were no respirators to pump fresh air into the confined spaces in which we worked. The welding torches created a choking, acrid smoke that filled what little air we had and stung our eyes and noses. After climbing out of the hull into the fresh air, we coughed up black mucus from deep in our lungs. Nobody questioned the circumstances, though. The newspapers were filled with reports of merchant freighters being sunk by German submarines. The country was gearing up. We needed Liberty Ships, and we couldn't build them fast enough.

The flip side of the uncomfortable working conditions, of course, was the pay. I made twice as much at the shipyards as I would have logging. I lived in a nice boarding house, had plenty of pocket money and, true to the formula, I spent eight hundred dollars and bought a brand new 1940 Ford. Every few weeks I drove my new car down the valley, had a visit at home, and a couple of dates with a pretty girl named Faye. By this time, my younger brother Maury was a private in the Army, Gene was still working in the woods, and our youngest brother, Loyd, was still in high school. Things were going well enough.

Then Pearl Harbor happened and I knew that one way or the other I'd soon be in uniform. The lines in front of the recruiting centers stretched for blocks. It seemed that every young man in America was standing in line to enlist. I had tremendous respect for the men who served in all branches of the service, and I was charged with patriotism, but tromping around in the mud and being screamed at, for a piddling twenty-one dollars a month, didn't sound too appealing to me. I knew I didn't want to be in the "walking Army." But there was that old dream. Maybe I could fly.

At that time, there was no Air Force, per se. The Air Corps was still a branch of the Army. To be considered for flying school, you were supposed to have two years of college which, of course, I didn't have. But there was a test you could take to waive the college requirement. I was determined to pass that test. I'd always taken school pretty seriously, and even though I'd spent much of my youth attending a one-room schoolhouse, I felt that I'd received a good education through high school. I knew I could learn the material for the test if someone would just point me in the right direction.

I went to one of the local high schools near St. Johns, Oregon, and found two teachers who were willing to use their breaks between classes to tutor me in math and English. They never asked for compensation nor seemed to begrudge the extra time they gave me. In those days, it seemed that everyone wanted to do whatever possible to help the war effort. This was their way of pitching in.

For several weeks, I worked the night shift at St. Johns and studied during the day. Finally, I felt ready. Of course, I had to enlist to get the opportunity to take the test, but I wasn't alone. There were a lot of young men with the same idea. When I reported to the Portland Air Base to take the test, there were probably two hundred of us in the room. Tests had never made me especially nervous, and I don't recall worrying a lot about this one. I just went, took it, learned that I had passed, and that was that.

But I wasn't nearly so dispassionate about learning to fly. It was early 1942, I was twenty-three and an eager cadet in the Army Air Corps. I was ready to go. Curious. Excited. It was hard for me to visualize much of the reality of air warfare. My fantasies were filled instead with soaring and speed. I was going to fly! I couldn't wait.

But the Army wasn't ready for me yet. They had no place to send me or even a uniform I could wear. I got orders to report in six weeks. So I went home to my folks, worked in the woods a bit, and spent my spare time adding a second bedroom and a bathroom onto the little house my father had recently built. My mother, for the first time in her hard life, now lived in a house that had a bathroom with running water.

When my six weeks were up, I was sent to Fort Vancouver, Washington, where my orders, maddeningly, got me no closer to flying than guard duty and KP.

At last I was sent to preflight, or ground school, at San Antonio, Texas. Five thousand of us arrived at Randolph Field ready to become aviators. Upon graduation from ground school, each cadet would be classified to either continue in pilot training or to go to bombardier or navigator school.

Our days were an endless succession of classes and tests. We studied weather, Morse code, aircraft identification, and went through a series of automated tests that assessed eye-hand coordination and reaction speed. For aspiring pilots, these automated tests were as important as the book work, because no matter how well a cadet performed on the written tests, he didn't stand a chance of being a pilot if he didn't do well on the coordination assessments.

We marched everywhere. We marched to breakfast, we marched to exercise, we marched to class.

We also did hours of calisthenics and cross-country running. Thankfully, my years of logging, running up and down mountains all day to tie cables around logs, had prepared me well for this aspect of Army life. The other cadets often called me "Grandpa" because I was three to five years older than most of them. Still, I consistently outran most of the younger guys. But even that didn't make it fun.

We were at Randolph Field for about six weeks, living in tents pitched next to the airstrip. It was hot and dusty, with no trees in sight. If we wanted to sit down, we had to sit on the ground where the chiggers could feast on us. And for entertainment, it seemed that there was always a native Texan handy to boast about what a great state Texas was. I remained unconvinced.

There were dozens of trainer planes parked at the field. One morning, instead of the usual routine, we cadets were marched to the field and assigned to planes in groups of ten to fifteen. A hurricane was approaching and our orders were to stand out in the storm and physically hold the planes down when the storm hit. As we attached extra lines, the sky darkened and the wind picked up. We didn't have to wait long before the gale hit in full force.

Although it wasn't cold, the rain blew like sand and stung when it hit flesh. Battered by the high winds and soaked to the skin, we struggled with the planes for hours, trying to hold onto something that, by design, lifts in the wind. It was hard to see very far and we couldn't hear one another unless we stood close and shouted. Bareheaded and in shirtsleeves, struggling with the aircraft, each man waged his own small war with the storm. When the crisis was finally over, we dragged ourselves back to the tent area.

The tents had not stood up well in the hurricane. In fact, many had scudded before the storm like sailing schooners, trailing their cargo in a wake behind them. The belongings of five thousand tired, bedraggled men lay scrambled and waterlogged in the mud, tangled in a mess of tent poles, rope, and canvas. Rather than try to salvage any of the mess, the Army loaded us all into trucks and took us to temporary barracks at another field where we were re-issued everything from blankets and toothbrushes to writing paper. I remember thinking that I hadn't particularly cared for Texas when it was just dry, dusty, ugly, and hot. Now I liked it even less, and six weeks seemed like a long time to be forced to stay there.

Still on track for pilot training, my next stop was Chickasha, Oklahoma for primary school. There were probably two hundred cadets there at a time. Life at Chickasha was great. The school was a private flying school under contract to the Army. The instructors were all civilians, real nice people, and the school barracks were clean and modern. Almost plushy, in fact. The food was fantastic and they even had people come in to make our beds. It was like staying in a nice hotel, only more fun, because we were learning to fly.

We flew PT-19s; single engine primary trainers. These were 175hp, single engine two-seaters with an open cockpit. Simple little planes, they had fixed landing gear and a fixed pitch prop. The low wooden wings were attached to a fuselage that consisted of canvas stretched over a frame. The instructor, who sat in the front seat, communicated with the student through a rubber speaking tube. I remember how excited I was when I heard the instructor's voice come through that tube during our first time up. "Take the stick, Pickett." I couldn't believe I was really there.

Those planes were primitive, perhaps, but for me, flying them was my dream come true. Every time I got out of a plane, I couldn't wait until the next time I could get back in.

They really took us through our paces in primary. In four months we went from our first ride to doing snap rolls, slow rolls, inverted flight, and loops. They threw a lot at us, and we were expected to catch it. Fast.

If a cadet seemed a little slow, made too many mistakes, or was at all prone to airsickness, he was sent for a ride in the "Washing Machine." This plane belonged to the senior instructor who would make the final determination as to whether a struggling cadet could continue in the program or whether he would be "washed out." Few flyers passed, and although it usually took a few days to get new orders, they generally knew in a matter of hours whether they'd be staying.

The evaluation process was continual and strict. The Army wasn't interested in investing money in training a pilot if there was any doubt about whether he could handle a complicated aircraft in combat.

I was fortunate to have been assigned to a gem of an instructor. His name, I think, was Jake Lieb. Probably only five years older than I, Jake was short and cocky. To look at him, you might have thought he was just a rock-throwing farm boy, but he really knew how to turn an eager kid into a pilot.

Lieb was an extremely precise instructor. There was never any half-way or part-way about flying with Jake. He was particular, but we enjoyed ourselves at the same time. I soloed after only eight hours, compared to the twenty hours that an average private pilot might take today. All of Jake's students did well. I don't think that any of his four cadets washed out of primary in the four months we were there. Considering an attrition rate of what I am sure was somewhere between forty and sixty percent, that was quite an accomplishment.

One of our tests was called "jumping hurdles." The hurdle stage was a small grass airstrip on which they had erected a post-and-wire fence across the runway. The point of the exercise was to come in low, lift up to clear the fence and then make a three point landing, coming to a quick stop before a line marked across the field. It was a real finesse exercise, but Lieb took me out to practice the day before the test and really made it seem easy.

On the day of the test, the plan was that we would spend the day at the hurdle stage, all flying in a circle to come around for our turn. Once we stopped, we'd take right off again to get back in line to come around for another try. I thought this whole exercise was a lot of fun, and I nailed my first three tries. Right on the money. As I came to a stop on my third try, the instructor on the field motioned me off to the side.

"You can go on in for the rest of the day. Let someone else have your plane," he said. I was a little confused.

"Did I pass?" I asked.

"Pickett," he said, "I think you took the spots right off that plane. You passed." Even without the plane, I think I was soaring for hours. As I learned that night, several people never did manage to get it right that day. It sure made me appreciate Lieb.

Lieb also taught me the no-miss emergency landing. When you're flying along, nowhere near the field, and your instructor turns the engine off and says, "Land it," it's fairly certain you'll pay attention to his instructions. Again, Lieb made things easy. He gave me a few, simple, repeatable steps; something for my mind to hold onto when everything else in my body said to panic. First: find someplace that will serve as a field, keeping in mind not only size but texture. Second: determine wind direction. Third: glide to the downwind side of the field. Fourth: as you lose altitude, turn figure eights, always making the turns toward the field. Fifth: turn and drop, turn and drop, knowing that as soon as you hit the optimum altitude for putting down, you can stop anywhere in the figure eight to line up and land.

Lieb practiced with me, building my confidence. It's hard to describe my exhilaration when I passed my test with a flawless emergency landing. I've seen the same elation reflected on the faces of athletes when they've executed well under pressure, but still, there are few words to describe how I felt as I brought that plane to a stop. All I can say is that after more than fifty years, I can still look back and say to myself, "That was a good day."

At the end of primary school they sent us to basic training in

Waco, Texas. I was still holding a grudge against Texas, and basic training didn't do a thing to help me get over it. We were at an Army field this time and, as they enjoyed telling us, the country club was over.

The barracks were temporary wooden structures. With exposed studs and bare light bulbs, they were anything but homey. Heat was provided by coal stoves, one at each end of the room. There were probably forty cots, a few were made of wood, but most of them were metal.

Each cadet had a locker at the head of his cot and a trunk at the foot. Everything had to be arranged to exact specifications: the clothes in the locker had to be hung in a certain order and the socks in the trunk had to be rolled, toes together, with one cuff folded over top into a precisely measured square. In the morning, we had a specified number of minutes to perform each task: so many minutes to shave, so many minutes to shower, and so many minutes to prepare for inspection.

If, during inspection, an officer happened to toss a coin onto a cot, the blankets had to be taut enough that the coin bounced. Because making up the cots to specifications wasn't all that easy, it was common for men to sleep on top of the blankets at night.

We marched everywhere, of course. After inspection, we marched off to breakfast for our first meal of the day. The routine never varied. We always sat at the same table and in the same spot at that table. We were to sit only on the front four inches of our chairs, very erect, no talking, no smoking, no looking around.

The food was excellent. We usually had some kind of steak or roast beef with a nice salad and dessert. We passed the food around the table from right to left. While passing the food, our eyes were to remain looking straight ahead. If we cared to have bread, we were to break it into four equal rectangles and stack them at a specific point on the side of our plate. We were to butter only one rectangle at a time and, needless to say, nobody mopped up his gravy with it.

Getting food into our mouths was a study in right angles. Truly, a "square meal." The fork was to be lifted vertically from the plate until it was at mouth level. Then, moving parallel to the table, it was brought to the mouth. The route back to the plate was the same thing in reverse.

Basic training lasted four months and every day brought a new threat of washing out. We continued with ground school and the flying was tougher. We flew bigger planes, 450hp BT-13s. These planes had an all-metal fuselage with a canopy you pulled over the top after climbing in. Although they still had fixed landing gear, they had a two-stage prop. We did a lot of formation flying and more intricate aerobatics. Although I had good instruction, basic was a time of constant worry for me. I thought that any day I might wash out. It was such a relief when it was finally over and I had passed.

Ernest Pickett and a BT-13 during basic training in Waco, Texas.

Upon graduation from basic, we were told to indicate whether we wanted to go to multi-engine school or to single-engine school. For me, it was an easy choice; I was drawn to the bigger planes. I liked that they had more engines and could stay in the air longer than the three or four hours a fighter could stay aloft and I liked the idea of being part of a crew. Also, my brother Maury was serving as a gunner on a B-17 crew in England. Although he was a world away, this choice somehow made him seem less distant.

Advanced training for multi-engines was also at Waco, although at a different field. They were "all Army" here, too. My instructor, 1st Lt. Youngblood, was tough. Tall and fair-haired, he was very military. His uniform, unfailingly, was pressed and crisp with the brass polished to perfection.

Impeccably polite, he was nevertheless demanding. If we made a little mistake, he didn't hesitate to dress us down. I liked him. He was a first-rate pilot and an excellent instructor. He was 23, as was I.

Beyond the constant threat of washing out, advanced training held an additional worry for me. My name was drawn as squadron commander. Although the impressive title would lead one to think that this was some kind of honor, the squadron commander was really just the poor guy who took the rap for everything that went wrong in the barracks. The only thing I did to earn the designation was that, when they assigned the bunks in alphabetical order, I happened to draw the first bunk in my barracks.

As squadron commander, my life became one of constant vigilance. Was this guy ever going to learn to roll his socks right? Was that bed made snugly enough? Fortunately, the other men in the barracks were devoted to these details, too. Any indiscretion was punishable by a gig, meaning that you and your squadron commander got to spend an hour with parachutes strapped on your backs, marching up and down the ramp—the taxiway alongside the airstrip. The gig itself wasn't all that fun, but the worst part was that you had to do your gig on the day the rest of the men went to town.

I didn't see much of the town of Waco after one particular incident, although in this case my punishment had nothing to do with my being squadron commander. We had some hot little twin-engine planes for advanced training: AT-9s, AT-10s and AT-17s. The AT-9s and 10s were the fastest. They had lots of horsepower and variable speed props, and we loved to make them go.

We soloed in pairs, one student serving as pilot, the other as co-pilot, and then we'd switch. The roles in the two seats were highly defined. When landing, the pilot gave a signal and the co-pilot lowered the flaps. When taking off, the pilot gave a signal and the co-pilot raised the landing gear.

On our first solo flight, my partner and I were doing touch and go landings; that is, we'd come in and touch down, then go right back up and come around again. On one approach, I was in the pilot seat and gave the signal, but the co-pilot hit the wrong switch, thereby raising the landing gear instead of the flaps. The plane skidded down the runway on her belly, out of control, with two horrified young men inside.

We did a lot of gigs for that mishap. And, reminiscent of grade school, we wrote sentences: "The landing gear switch is on the left side of the control module. The flap switch is on the right side of the control module," copying each sentence five or six hundred times.

Although the incident wasn't directly my fault, it carried a powerful lesson: the pilot is ultimately responsible for the lives of his crew. It is a lesson that, as things turned out later, has never ceased to haunt me.

Airborne!

*"Very few, there were, among the officers, who had not passed prelimi-
nary inspection by some trusted "scout" of General Wolfe and his staff.
In short, the personnel of the 58th Wing, from Colonels to Corporals,
was as nearly "hand-picked" as it very will (sic) could be—under strict
Army Regulations."*

History of the 58th Bomb Wing (H)
declassified by HQ USAFHRC
DOD DIR 5200.9 27 Sep 58
regarding the selection of the first B-29 personnel

Upon qualification from advanced training school, I was allowed to choose which type of multi-engine plane I wanted to fly.
Essentially, there were four categories: two-engine and four-engine
combat aircraft, and two-engine and four-engine cargo and troop
transports. Some of us were even allowed to choose the specific
plane.

I wanted to fly B-24s. Named the Liberator, B-24s were four-
engine heavy bombers. Although they couldn't fly as high as the
B-17 Flying Fortresses, which made them more susceptible to flak
and fighters, they were much faster and could carry more bombs. I
was assigned to B-24 transition school at Davis-Monthan Air Field
in Tucson in preparation for being sent overseas with a crew.

Before reporting to transition school, though, we were given a
short leave. I boarded a train from Waco, Texas, to Oregon, eager to
get home. My parents met me at the station in Albany as planned,

15

but had some unexpected bad news. They had received a telegram that my leave had been cancelled and that I was to report to Tucson immediately. I got on the next southbound train having had only a brief visit with my folks at the station. I certainly wasn't looking forward to another couple of days confined to a train.

When I reached Tucson, I was told that there had been a mistake in the orders and that I was, indeed, on leave. Back to the train station and another long trip to Oregon. This time, I stayed. My time at home was especially pleasant. I had been dating Faye Gedney for over a year, exchanging letters while I'd been gone, not sure how serious I was ready to get. During this leave I realized how much I had missed her, and had it not been for the war, I would have proposed. We both knew I'd soon be headed overseas and it was hard to say goodbye.

In transition school, all the roles in performing missions came together. We were assigned crews and spent endless hours performing mock bomb runs from various altitudes, dropping smoke bombs onto small wooden shacks the Army had erected in the desert. We also did a lot of gunnery practice and high-altitude flying. We practiced landings with just two or three engines. And, although we had done plenty of night flying in our previous training, we now did formation flying at night.

Formation flying at night was hard because the only way to know the position of the other planes was to watch the blue formation lights that were mounted on the exterior of the planes. Because bright lights would make us easy targets on a mission, the formation lights were intentionally dim. We had to stay in close just to know where the other planes were. Of course, being young, I didn't dwell on thoughts of mid-air collisions. I just got into formation and flew. Piece of cake.

I had a good crew in Tucson. We performed well and got along with each other. At last, we got our orders for North Africa. We had our shots and had been processed for departure when, on the day before we were to leave, the Army pulled me off the crew, issued orders for me to stay in Tucson as an instructor, and assigned another pilot to my crew. I hated to see the guys go. We were a great team and good friends. I was upset at being all ready to go and then have everything change at the last minute. I learned after the war, when I ran into two of the gunners in a hospital, that the crew was eventually shot down. Aside from the two gunners I saw, only the navigator survived. They had been POWs in Germany.

Being an instructor was grueling duty. We kept a four hours on/four hours off schedule around the clock with one day off per week. In the four hours we had off, we had to eat, sleep, take care of personal details like brushing teeth, shaving, showering, and letter-writing. And, of course, when we reported again in four hours we were expected to look crisp, pressed, and spotless. Sleep was at a premium. We ached for it.

We didn't know then that our need for sleep was due to an oxygen depletion problem as much as it was due to our round-the-clock work rotation. At that time, the Army thought that oxygen was only needed above 10,000 feet. While that was true during the day, we didn't know that the ceiling dropped to 8,000 feet at night. We did a lot of high-altitude night flying in Tucson, and because of it we were in a state of constant exhaustion, tiring easily. We became lethargic and dull. It wasn't until later, when the Army learned that the oxygen levels changed at night and had duplicated some captured German technology, that oxygen depletion became less of an issue for American flyers.

Sleep and heat were our preoccupations. When we did manage to lie down to catch a couple hours of rest during the day, we were in a barracks that lay baking under the Tucson sun. There was no shade and no air conditioning. All we could do was lie on our bunks and sweat.

To make matters worse, the high-altitude flying meant that we had to wear oxygen masks and heavy fleece-lined flight suits. Climbing into one of those warm leather suits in summer in the desert was a real exercise in willpower, but we did it, time and time again.

I figured that I was going to be an instructor for a long time, so finally I wrote to Faye and proposed. To my delight, she said, "Yes," and we began to make arrangements for her to meet me in Tucson to get married.

Two or three weeks before she was due to arrive, however, my orders suddenly changed. The wedding would have to be postponed. Tucson was closed as a transition school and the instructors ferried the planes to Orlando. The instructors weren't transferred with the planes, though. Instead, we were loaded onto a troop train and sent to Great Bend, Kansas. They told us we'd be in Great Bend for about a year, but they didn't tell us what we would be doing there. We heard only that we were going to be involved in a top-secret project which we were not to discuss even with our families.

When we arrived at Great Bend, there was no train station and no transportation. We unloaded our belongings, formed ranks, and marched the mile to the airfield. There we found temporary single-wall barracks with tarpaper tacked on the outside, and the widest, longest, runways we had ever seen. The airfield was obviously brand new and was built to accommodate something special.

We soon learned that we had been sent there to form a new group, the 444th. We would belong to the 58th Bomb Wing of the Twentieth (XX) Bomber Command. The Army was coming out with the B-29 Superfortress, a new long-range bomber, and we, members of the newly activated Twentieth Air Force, were going to be the first to take it overseas.

The early B-29s were still in production when we first arrived in Kansas and at first there wasn't even a plane available for us to look at, let alone fly. We focused on book work, learning all we could about this complex new plane.

But then one day, two full colonels flew a B-29 in to the Great Bend Army Air Field. It was one of the first out of the factory. We could hardly believe our eyes. It was huge, twice the size of a B-24. We stood on the ground looking at it, absolutely awe-struck.

"That thing'll never fly," one fella remarked.

"Well, if it does," someone answered, "you can't take it into a steep turn. All the water will spill out of the swimming pool."

The colonels took some of the pilots—the captains and majors—on familiarization flights. The enormous Plexiglas greenhouse which comprised the nose of the craft took some getting used to. We were up higher and back farther from the nose than we had ever been before. Instead of the co-pilot sitting right next to the pilot, it felt as if the seats were across a room from one another. Because the pilot seat was so far to the left of center, we took a man on those early flights just to sit between the pilot and co-pilot and shout adjustments to keep the nose-wheel on the center line during taxi and takeoff. To my delight, even though I probably got the job only because I was a lowly 2nd lieutenant, I got to go on several flights during the colonels' visit to serve this function.

Our own planes were very slow in coming. The B-29 had gone from drawing board to full production in record time. Still, they didn't arrive fast enough for the Army. This plane was the American hope for taking the war to the Japanese homeland. The feeling was, that the sooner it was deployed, the sooner the war would be over. The early planes were full of problems and the engineers worked out all kinds of kinks as we learned how to handle the planes. There was a real sense of urgency about making the program a success and, despite the many glitches in the first models, we eventually won what would go down in history as The Battle of Kansas.

At the time, the B-29 was the most sophisticated airplane to have ever been built. Costing over a million dollars, it had a wing span of 141 feet and four 2200hp engines. A B-29 could carry four times the bomb load of a B-17 and could fly, not only farther and higher, but faster than most fighters. With the bombs, ammunition and fuel expended after a mission, it cruised at 300mph. Fully loaded, it weighed 140,000 pounds and consumed 640 gallons of fuel an hour in takeoff and climb. Designed for long-range missions, it could stay airborne for nineteen hours.

The on-board electro-mechanical computers and complex management of the various systems on the craft required a dedicated flight engineer who concentrated on keeping the load balanced as the aircraft consumed the enormous quantities of fuel that kept it aloft for such long periods of time. The wing tanks alone could hold 5400 gallons, and on long missions, three tanks hung in the enormous forward bomb bay, each holding 640 gallons of fuel. Except for the flight controls, all controls on the plane were electric. Only the brakes were hydraulic, and even they had electric backup.

One of the major improvements over the other bombers in terms of crew comfort was the introduction of the pressurized cabin. Instead of wearing heavy fleece-lined suits and oxygen masks that could freeze to their faces, the crew wore state-of-the-art electric flight suits that plugged into sockets at their stations to keep them warm if the plane lost pressure. And, of course, there were oxygen masks handy if needed.

In an airplane which seemed so large from the outside, very little space was used by the crew who manned it. It was evident from the design that every last aspect of the plane was determined by the goal of delivering the largest possible payload to the farthest possible target without losing the plane. Aside from pressurization—and the electric food warmers, installed both front and rear that enabled us to have hot meals on long missions—very little consideration was given to crew comfort. The only seat cushions were the seat-pack parachutes the crew wore over their flight suits.

The crew compartments were divided into two main areas, the forward pressure cabin and the rear—or aft—pressure cabin, located midship behind the rear bomb bay. The tail gunner had a separate tiny pressurized compartment in the very back of the plane facing backward. The pilot, co-pilot, flight engineer, bombardier, navigator and radio operator occupied the forward pressure cabin. Later in the war, the pilot would be referred to as the aircraft commander, and the co-pilot would be renamed pilot.

The bombardier sat in the nose of the plane, ahead of and below the pilot's instrument panel, while the navigator sat behind the pilot on the left of the plane, and the flight engineer sat behind the co-pilot on the right. The radio operator sat aft of the flight engineer. The rear pressure cabin was occupied by three gunners, two of whom sat at Plexiglas bubbles, one on either side of the plane. The senior gunner sat in what looked like a swivel barber chair beneath a blister on the top of the plane, just above the side gunners. Later, when radar was added, the radar operator was also stationed in the rear cabin.

The B-29 was the first plane to regularly carry on-board radar. While some of the earliest models did not come equipped with it, ours did. It was the first plane in our squadron to come from the factory with radar installed, but we didn't have a radar operator until we got overseas. Eventually, all of the planes had radar. This tool became especially important later during missions over the Himalayas when bad weather made seeing the deadly mountains almost impossible.

The crew communicated primarily over an intercom. While there was a narrow, pressurized tunnel above the bomb bays, connecting the two main cabins, it was a long, hard crawl to move from one to the other, and one had to take off his parachute to do it.

Also, if one of the pressurized cabins happened to lose pressure while someone was in the tunnel, the force of the air moving through the tunnel between the unpressurized and pressurized area would eject him from the tunnel like a shot from a cannon, with almost certain fatal results. For the most part, everyone remained at his station during a flight and the passageway was used only during emergencies.

Because the B-29 would typically be flying without the benefit of fighter cover, it was imperative that it be able to defend itself against enemy attack. The plane was heavily armored. Bullet-resistant glass was mounted above the pilot and co-pilot's instrument panels, and floor-to-ceiling sheets of 3/8" armor plate were at their backs. The fuel tanks had a special self-sealing inner lining that prevented them from leaking or exploding if struck.

The crew included four gunners plus a bombardier who doubled as a gunner in the nose. Unlike the earlier bombers where the side gunners opened a hatch in the side of the plane, pointed the gun and fired, the B-29 had central, computerized fire control. The four huge electric-powered gun turrets were mounted well away from the gunners, two on the top of the plane, two on the bottom. Each turret had a 360-degree field of fire and held ten fifty-caliber machine guns. The nose gunner (bombardier), senior gunner and two side gunners shared the four gun turrets between them, firing by remote control. The senior gunner reached his station via a narrow ladder in the rear pressure cabin. In his bubble on top of the plane, the senior gunner could literally rotate his chair to see 360 degrees around, and anywhere above the plane. From his vantage point, he was an incredibly efficient defender.

The senior gunner orchestrated which gunner had control of each of the four turrets at any particular time. This way, he could make optimal use of each gunner's unique field of vision and he could keep all of the guns firing in response to the direction and intensity of attack. Each gunner's sight was linked to the central fire control system, so it automatically adjusted to the locations and angles of the different guns.

The computer-assisted gun sights worked roughly as follows: The gunner looked through the sight, saw and recognized a target. From memory, the gunner entered the wing span of the target aircraft, and adjusted the diameter of a reticle of lights in his gun sight to the wingspan of the target. At the same time, the navigator was continually updating the on-board computer with information about temperature, altitude and air speed. As the gunner watched the target through the gun sight, he waited until the outline of the wings lined up on the reticle, and then fired. The sights were remarkably accurate.

The side gunners, perched at the blisters on the sides of the plane, were possibly the most vulnerable of all the members of the crew. There were instances, once the B-29s got into combat, where the side blisters blew out, and the gunners were sucked out of the plane. I heard one account after the war of a gunner who had had such a vivid nightmare of that happening to him, that he devised a harness for himself prior to his next mission. Sure enough, his bubble blew out and he was sucked out of the plane. He dangled there helplessly for nearly an hour, but finally his crewmates were able to haul him back in, frost-bitten and shaken, but alive, by the lead he had attached to his harness.

The tail gunner was the most isolated and the most cramped of the crew. He entered his tiny compartment at the extreme rear of the plane via a crawlway from the rear main door. As soon as the plane was pressurized he had to sit, essentially unmoving, for the duration of the flight. Facing aft, he had perhaps six inches of leeway on either side of his shoulders. In front of him were two 50-caliber automatic machine guns and between his feet was a 20-millimeter cannon. To sight the cannon, the tail gunner watched the tracers from his machine guns. When the tracers went into the target, he could reach down between his feet and fire. While the overall effectiveness of the cannon has been debated, there is no doubt that it added to the already imposing appearance of the enormous plane.

The main defensive weakness of the B-29 was eventually discovered by one of Japan's greatest Zeros who shot down twenty-seven B-29s. His secret? He approached them from below. While there were guns mounted on the bottom of the plane, the gunners did not have an adequate field of vision to use them effectively to ward off such attacks.

While the pilot, co-pilot, navigator, gunners, and radio and radar operators worked to get the plane over the target, there was one man whose primary role on a many-houred mission lasted only a few minutes. This man was the bombardier. It was his job to get the bombs on the target. To do this, he used one of the most sophisticated pieces of equipment available at the time, the Norden bombsight. Sitting seemingly suspended in the Plexiglas nose of the plane, with Plexiglas beneath and around him, the bombardier had optimum visibility for orienting himself and recognizing the target as the plane approached. Although the bomb release mechanisms could be set for incremental release, according to mission orders, the bombardier was in charge of initiating the release. This was done by remote control, as was the opening of the bomb bay doors.

The bombardier fed information into the bombsight, including type of bomb, air speed, temperature, altitude, wind speed and direction, which enabled the bombsight to calculate the precise instant at which the bombs should be released. In the final moments of the bomb run, the pilot put the aircraft on autopilot, which automatically responded to corrections entered into the bombsight. This gave the bombardier control over all the possible variables via the bombsight, and increased bombing accuracy immensely—some said to within a 100-foot circle from four miles up.

Before the B-29, it was also the bombardier's job to arm the bombs en route to the target. Because B-29 bomb bays were not pressurized and because the bombardier no longer had easy access to the bays, the Army developed self-arming bombs. On the nose of each bomb was a little propeller. As the bomb dropped, the propeller spun in the wind and eventually unscrewed, thereby arming the bomb as it fell toward the target.

In all, when radar was added, it took eleven men to crew a B-29. With the addition of the maintenance and support staff it took to keep it airborne, each plane was a big operation.

As the 58th Wing grew in size and more personnel came into the program, we began to split off to form new groups. About a month after we all arrived in Great Bend, half of us were moved to Smokey Hill Air Field, in Salina, Kansas, to form the 468th Bombardment Group.

While I was still in Great Bend, however, Faye and I decided to go ahead with the wedding. I had heard that it might be a year before the planes and crews were ready, so I called her and told her to get on a train for Big Bend, Kansas. After figuring out that there was no Big Bend, and that I really wanted her to show up in Great Bend, she swung into action. In a couple short weeks she had quit her job as a teller at a bank and had been given wedding showers by friends and church members. Leaving most of her belongings behind, she packed two suitcases and headed toward Kansas.

When she arrived on the morning of August 8, 1943, I was there to meet her in a borrowed car. There was no station at Great Bend, so I picked her up in Hutchinson, Kansas, about eleven miles away. The train was several hours late, and you'd think that sitting there, I would have had time to get nervous. But I wasn't nervous. I couldn't wait to see Faye. I hadn't seen her in about four months, and when she stepped off the train, I nearly popped. I was so happy to see her.

Being summer in Kansas, it was already warm, and Faye had been on the train for most of three days. She had to have been hot and tired, but for some reason one of the first things out of my mouth when I saw her was, "We're going to buy you a fur coat." She must have thought I was nuts and seemed a little relieved to hear that I didn't mean "right now."

I had picked up our marriage license earlier and made arrangements with the minister of the Christian Church to perform the ceremony for us at one o'clock at the parsonage. I still remember the minister's name: James Behler. My buddy, Al Reida, and his wife Sirrkka had agreed to stand up with us as our witnesses.

We didn't have much time to get ready, so we drove to our hotel in Great Bend and I called Sirrkka to come help Faye press her clothes and get dressed. I wore my dress uniform and Faye looked absolutely gorgeous in a pale blue suit. Aside from Al and Sirrkka, there were no guests, but the pastor's wife had an organ in the parsonage and played some music to make it nicer. At the end of the ceremony, the preacher's wife turned to Faye and said, "Congratulations, Mrs. Pickett." Boy, was I happy.

After the ceremony, we took Al and Sirrkka out to a late lunch. It had not been a traditional wedding day, but if Faye was disappointed by not having her friends and family present, she never showed it.

She also didn't seem too disappointed by our first dinner as a married couple. I had commented to her during the day that she was much too thin and I had made a big point of how I was going to make sure she ate three full meals a day. Unfortunately, by the time we were ready to go to dinner that night, all the restaurants in Great Bend were closed and we ended up having a milkshake at the

Walgreens soda fountain.

I had stressed to Faye that she had to travel light and that she could not bring more to Kansas than she could fit into two suit-cases, and so, naturally, she had left her nice wedding gifts at home. Therefore, the next day we went to the five-and-dime store and bought two plates, two cups, two bowls, a couple of pans and some cheap wood-handled utensils and moved into our little motel/cabin apartment right across the street from the Reidas.

It was incredibly small. The entire kitchen and dining area was no larger than an average dining room table. A narrow little table folded down from the wall and was just large enough to hold our plates and a couple of glasses. Once behind it, the only way to get past it was to fold it back up. Because there was no room for serving dishes, and because we didn't own any, Faye served from the stove.

It couldn't have been an easy place for Faye to practice her homemaking skills. The first few weeks held their share of kitchen catastrophes. She unknowingly bought field corn at the market in-stead of sweet corn and cooked it over and over again in frustra-tion, trying to make it taste cooked instead of raw. And, because there had been no room in her suitcase for her recipe books, she had to try whatever recipes she could get hold of. One lemon me-ringue pie was especially memorable. It was impossible to tell where the crust left off and the pan began.

I probably had a little to learn about being a sensitive hus-band. I recall one evening that Faye was dishing up the plates as I maneuvered into position at the table. She had served hers and placed it on the table. When she reached across with mine, how-ever, she dropped it. The plate crashed to the floor and broke into pieces. Of course, now we had only one plate to eat from, so with-out missing a beat, I simply reached over, took her plate and dug in. To my amazement, my young, pretty twenty-year-old bride burst into tears.

Soon after our wedding, we and the Reidas decided to pool our money and buy a car. It was an old Terraplane that had traded hands a couple of times on the base and was known by all as "The Green Peril." We had to stop every ten miles to put in oil or water. At first, I wasn't going to let Faye drive it, but when someone was needed to go apartment-hunting in preparation for our move to Salina, and Sirrka didn't drive, Al insisted that, "Faye can do it." I relented. She managed fine and we ended up with an apartment.

There was a tremendous housing shortage. Salina was a small town and not at all prepared for the influx of personnel at the base. We were fortunate to find a nice couple, Richard and Ollie Cowie, who rented the basement of their home to the Reidas and us. It had two bedrooms, a shared kitchen, and a little shower in the laundry room.

On the day we moved to Salina, Al and I used "The Peril" to take one or two loads of belongings to the new place and then went back for the last load and the girls. We piled bedding in the back seat and Faye and I climbed in on top of it. The car was loaded to the max and died about three blocks from the new apartment. While Al stepped out to figure out what had gone wrong this time, I started looking around at the car. I noticed a little hole in the headliner just above me. Bored, I turned to Faye and said, "I wonder what would happen if I stuck my little finger in this hole," and did. The entire ceiling came crashing down covering Sirrka, Faye, me, and all of our belongings in dust.

I was still intent on buying Faye that fur coat I had promised her. So, sometime in September or October we went shopping and came home with a muskrat coat that fell to just below her knees. Winters in Kansas can be brutal and she wore it a lot when the temperatures dropped.

Because there were still no B-29s available after we moved to Salina, we got six new B-26s so we could start logging some hours. Later, they brought in several old B-17s, too. The B-26s were especially valuable to us because they had the tricycle landing gear most similar to what the B-29s would have and, like a B-29, they came in real fast on the landings.

B-26s were shaped like a long, smooth cigar. I liked the look of them and the way they flew, but a lot of the boys hated them. The problem was that B-26s, which had only two engines to begin with, were subject to frequent engine failure. Losing an engine on takeoff in a B-26 could be pretty scary. We had heard that there had been many fatal crashes at the B-26 school in Florida.

Having fiddled with lots of different engines at home, I was pretty sure that the problem with the B-26 engines was that the spark plugs were getting fouled from the engine being idled too long before takeoff. I felt that the way to avoid a problem was to always get the plane into position as quickly as possible and get her rolling down the runway. I made it a practice to do just that.

I flew with a lot of different men before we got our final crew assignments and I noticed an interesting phenomenon in at least four or five of my co-pilots when we were assigned to a B-26. Each young man would be visibly nervous as we went through our pre-flight checklist, and as we'd get closer to takeoff, I'd glance at my co-pilot and see sweat pouring in sheets from the top of his head and down his face. Naturally, I'd try to be reassuring, but I think the guys tended to put more stock in the rumors from Florida than they did my spark plug theory.

I remember flying with one co-pilot who made it very clear that he didn't want to be on that plane. He had broken into the characteristic sweat and was choking down panic. I finally got a little impatient with him. I told him, "Just read the checklist and let's get this thing off the ground."

Of course, we were fine. I never had a problem with a B-26. In fact, I really looked forward to flying them. They handled well and were fast compared to the other planes. We were told that the glide path was similar to that of the B-29. We had to bring them in at 120mph to keep the engines from stalling, so the landings were fast and fun.

The Army was anxious that we get as many hours under our belts as we could while we waited for our B-29s to arrive. If we could come up with any reasonable-sounding purpose to fly somewhere, we were given a plane. What a great situation. Available planes and time to fly them. I was in heaven.

For the most part, I was an extremely serious, conscientious pilot. Even on the ground, I wasn't real big on mischief. I certainly wasn't known for drinking or carousing. But I did pull a couple of pranks while out in those B-26s, racking up those hours. I wasn't too proud of my antics, even at the time, but some of the fellas who were riding with me sure enjoyed them.

The first one, I recall, began innocently. One of the men on the crew was from Colorado and was pretty homesick. He asked if we could fly over his parents' ranch just so he could see it. The trip was pretty uneventful until we got him over familiar territory. He was so excited to see home that I decided to take him in a little closer. I dropped altitude and circled around, verifying that the spread up ahead was his. It was, and I just kept dropping. We decided we ought to buzz the place to say hello to the folks. I looked at the barn and the house and decided that I could probably get that plane right in between them. And I did. I threaded the needle.

When we got back to the base, the guy called his folks. His mother asked, "Son, was that you in that plane?" When she heard his enthusiastic reply, she said seriously, "Son, don't you ever do that again." I never heard the details of the havoc we caused on that farm, but I'm sure we did more than rattle a few windows.

Another incident could have ended my career. My crew that day included some avid baseball fans. They were wistfully talking about how great it would be to see the World Series game being played that day in St. Louis. A little flyover seemed in order. We didn't have anywhere else to go. As you might guess, it was pretty tempting to go in for a closer look, and we did. We buzzed the World Series. One of the crew members listened to the game broadcast as we came in. He could hear the broadcasters saying "It looks like a B-26..." Fortunately, we were going much too fast for anyone to read the ID numbers.

At the time the group moved to Salina, only officers with a rank of captain or above were assigned to pilot B-29s. I believe most of them had combat experience, too. As a 2nd lieutenant, it was a given that I would be a co-pilot. I was delighted to learn that I had been assigned as co-pilot to the squadron commander, Lt. Colonel James Edmundson. He was an excellent officer and well-respected by the men, most of whom referred to him affectionately as "Colonel Jim." I felt privileged to fly with him.

National Archives

I had only flown with Colonel Edmundson for a short while before he turned to me one day and said, "Pickett, I'm going to check you out and give you a crew." And he did. He promoted me to 1st lieutenant. and I became a pilot. He did this with one other man, my friend, Al. We were the only 1st Lieutenants in the group to have crews.

James V. Edmundson, affectionately known as "Colonel Jim" to the 468th.

I had a dandy crew. With the exception of our excellent co-pilot, Ray Tolzmann, who was transferred to help out another crew just before we left for overseas, our crew stayed intact as originally assigned. They were, aside from myself and Ray:

Navigator: Harry "Hank" Robins
Bombardier: Ed 'Bud' Roberts
Flight Engineer: Mark Kennard
Radio Operator: Chuck Kazarian
Right Gunner: Dick Bishop
Senior Gunner: Bob Armstrong
Left Gunner: Sam Henry
Tail Gunner: Sam Nixon

To a man, these were great fellows. Ranging in age, probably from twenty to twenty-five, we came from all over the country and from a variety of backgrounds. Many had been to college a couple of years. Despite the differences, we became a tight-knit group and really enjoyed each other.

Bud Roberts, the bombardier, and his wife, Betty, got along with everyone. They loved to go to the Officers' Club to dance and socialize. They became good friends with Robins and his wife, who were both pretty quiet as a rule. I always had the impression that the Robinses came from a wealthy background. Hank was a top-notch navigator and there were many times I was grateful for his ability.

Kennard, our extremely capable flight engineer, wasn't one to pass up a drink, and could recite Robert Service poems from memory. He had been a master sergeant in the regular Army, but as a result of his B-29 training and position, he was now a flight officer. Because of this, he enjoyed a special status among the enlisted men. He could go to either the EM (Enlisted Men's) or to the Officers' Club to socialize.

Chuck Kazarian was another terrific guy. Wiry and olive-skinned, he was warm and friendly, always ready with a smile. To put it in the plainest terms, he was really a nice person. He was also an extremely conscientious and able radio operator.

Sam Nixon, our tail gunner, was a tall Kansas boy from Salina. I remember his mother as a very religious woman who was thrilled to have her son stationed, at least temporarily, so close to home.

Dick Bishop, our right gunner, was a natural leader. His stocky frame exuded confidence. He was serious, and took his responsibilities to heart. He was a little older than the rest of the crew, and he pretty much took charge of the enlisted men. He was originally from Michigan, I believe. Besides being a tremendous asset to the

Crew of the Reddy Teddy. Back row: Ernie Pickett, pilot; Bill Rewitz, co-pilot; Bud Roberts, bombardier; Hank Robins, navigator; Mark Kennard, flight engineer. Front row: Chuck Kazarian, radio operator; Shorty Armstrong, senior gunner; Dick Bishop, right gunner, Sam Nixon, tail gunner. Not shown: Sam Henry, left gunner; Bob Humphrey, radar operator who joined the crew in India; Ray Tolzmann, original co-pilot for the crew.

crew, he was also a good, honest, steady guy.

Sam Henry, our left gunner, tended to the quiet side and was a wonderful person. Of medium build and sandy-haired, he and Dick Bishop had gone to mechanic's school together and were close friends.

We called our senior gunner, Bob Armstrong, "Shorty" for reasons that were obvious if you stood next to him. Shorty was from Texas, but unlike his Texan compatriots I'd met in San Antonio, Shorty was a non-bragging Texan. I was relieved to finally meet someone from that state who wasn't annoying!

As a group, we had a lot of great adventures together. And of course, training and flying together, we came to know one another well. It was not part of military practice at that time for officers and enlisted men to socialize. In Kansas, we observed this unspoken rule, and in fact, I don't think the officers' wives and enlisted men's wives even met. But when we were alone, away from the base, our crew tended to do things together.

On one of our overnight cross-country trips, we all went to a carnival. Shorty was a good ballplayer, and at the carnival was a booth where you threw baseballs at milk bottles and got a prize if you knocked them all down. Shorty was a dead aim and threw the ball really hard. He didn't miss one. I got such a kick out of watching him that I started buying the tickets just to keep him throwing. Most of the crew was crowded around watching, cheering him on. Shorty just kept hammering them in there. The vendor was soon beside himself, and the longer we stayed, the more furious he became. Shorty won so many prizes that the vendor finally threatened to shut down the booth.

Of course, not all of our adventures were necessarily pleasant. One time, some of the wives met us in Oklahoma City. Three or four couples of us were out sightseeing and got on a crowded bus. Being from the Northwest, Faye and I had no idea that buses were segregated at that time, nor did most of the other people in the group. The only open seats were at the very back, so we all just hopped into the empty seats and continued on our merry way. Before long, we stopped again and an extremely heavy woman, whom we would now describe as African-American, got on and began working her way to the back of the bus. When she got to us, she looked around for an empty seat and, not finding one, sat down right on top of Kennard's wife, Rue V.. Now, Rue V. was from Texas, and she and Kennard, by rights, should have kept us out of those seats to begin with. But rather than apologize, or try to remedy the situation at all, Rue V. exploded.

Before the rest of us could even begin to grasp the situation, we found ourselves in the middle of a near riot. The two women started yelling at each other and Kennard had jumped into the fray, too. The rest of us did what we could to get Mark and Rue V. to calm down, and eventually, seeing no alternative, we decided to just get off the bus, hauling them along with us. The storm eventually blew over, and we resumed our tour, but the rest of us had learned something new about the South and race relations.

At some point during that trip, most of the crew and the wives went to the Ice Follies. We had decided to meet in the lobby of the hotel and go together. Faye was not only beautiful, of course, but was as nice a person then as she is today. The men seemed to genuinely like her, and I was always glad when she was with us. That night, as we waited for everyone to show up, in walked Shorty Armstrong with a bunch of sweet peas. He walked up to Faye and gave them to her explaining that he'd seen them and thought that she needed to have them. I think Shorty was single at the time, but there was no awkwardness about the exchange. It was simply a thoughtful gesture from one friend to another.

In addition to our crew members and the Reidas, I developed other close friendships during our time in Kansas. I became close to Major Brown, who first checked me out in B-17s before the B-29s arrived. When he got his plane, he named it "Chattanooga Choo-Choo." He was a special guy, and a really good instructor. I considered him a true soft-spoken Southern Gentleman.

James Pattillo, another pilot, was one of the most respected pilots in the group. He was considered a leader among the officers. I liked him a lot, and after the war he became a colonel and even did a stint at the Pentagon.

One of my closest friends was Dushan D. Ivanovich, pronounced Ivan-o-vik, with the emphasis on the "o." We had been instructors together in Tucson. He had black hair and a round face. Dark and handsome. Even though the women drooled, it didn't go to his head. He was a good-hearted guy, and our friendship meant a lot to me.

When Faye first came to Great Bend, Ivanovich gave her a wedding present. It was a Mexican white silver bracelet with a wide band made of dainty filigree rectangles. Obviously, he didn't have to give her a gift at all, but he wanted to give her something special to make her feel welcome.

During the ten months we were in Salina, we were busy and airborne much of the time. There still weren't enough B-29s to go around. For awhile there were only three or four planes per squadron of thirteen crews. There were four squadrons in a group and four groups in a wing. We were in the 792nd squadron. Eventually, we were able to share a plane between two crews. If we needed to go on a long-range ferrying mission, we almost always took a B-17. I imagine this was partly because it was less expensive for the Army, but also because the B-29 was still top-secret. It was no accident that our airfields were in the middle of the continent.

We did get in some longer flights in B-29s. Sometimes the Army needed to ferry planes between the factories in Witchita,

Seattle, and Marietta, Georgia, usually to deliver a new prototype. Our crew pulled this duty more than once. Naturally, we took a skeleton crew; we didn't need the gunners or bombardier over the United States. One time, though, we ferried a plane from Witchita to Marietta, packed with blueprints, and for some reason the whole crew got to go. That made it seem special. I enjoyed these trips in the B-29s. I couldn't believe how well they handled and I loved being in them.

When we ferried B-29s between factories, there was usually a B-17 along to transport the crew to the first factory and back from the delivery point. As other factories opened, such as the one in Omaha, we delivered prototypes there, as well.

It was common in the Army in those days for military planes to give service people a lift if they were going in the right direction. This could add days to the time a person actually got to spend at home on leave. In the case of a family emergency, people often headed to the nearest airfield to try to catch a ride cross-country.

Our group commander, Colonel Engler, had issued strict orders that none of our planes were to be used in this way under any circumstances. One time, though, when I was assigned to ferry a plane from Witchita to Marietta, I was approached by a master sergeant in the regular Army. He was desperate to get home to Florida. His dad was dying and he was worried he wouldn't get there in time. I could see that the guy was really upset and I wanted to help. I told him I could only get him halfway, to Marietta, and then I swore him to absolute secrecy. He wasn't to tell anyone, not even his family, how he had gotten home. Then we put him on the plane.

When we got to Georgia, I checked the flight line and found a plane slated for Florida. I looked up the pilot in his quarters and asked if he would take the guy with him. He agreed and I made the introductions. While I shouldn't have disobeyed orders, I felt that

I'd done the right thing.

Another time, I wasn't able to help someone who asked. A captain and I and our crews had flown two B-17s to New York City. I can still remember the night skyline as we descended. Everything about the city was huge—the massive docks, the endless miles of lights, and the towering skyscrapers. We flew in from the west, heading east, and turned south close to the Empire State Building and landed at Will Rogers Field.

We were headed to Seattle, and I was approached by a young lieutenant in the WAVEs who wanted to get a ride. She seemed really nice, but was extremely upset. Her dad was dying and she was desperate to get home. Of course as a 1st lieutenant traveling with a captain, the last thing I wanted to do was try to get away with taking someone on a plane against orders. I knew if he would go along with the idea, though, that it would be okay. He didn't.

He said he couldn't be bothered. We were both under orders, he told me. And of course, I knew that.

We left the girl behind. I felt so bad flying into Seattle, knowing that she could have been nearly home instead of stranded three thousand miles away.

Despite the orders that prohibited giving rides to military personnel, there were many times, however, when our orders were issued specifically to get people home. One time, when we were ferrying our B-24s from Tucson to Orlando before I entered the B-29 program, we even took a movie star, Robert Preston, with us. We picked him up in Orlando and he sat in the back and chatted with the other servicemen. Because the Army wanted us to log lots of flying time after we got to Kansas, we hauled a lot of people around the country.

Just before Christmas the year Faye and I were married, we were given leave and decided to go home to Oregon. The married men had their leaves early that year so they could return to Salina in time to fly the single men home for the holidays.

I was going to be flying a ferrying mission to Denver, so we decided to have Faye meet me there and we'd take the train home together, thereby getting us home a few days earlier. I put her on the train ahead of time, heading west. As a rule, the civilian trains were loaded beyond capacity, but this time it was especially bad. At first, keeping her suitcase with her, Faye and a sailor took turns alternately standing in the jammed aisle and sitting in one of the crowded seats. For most of the trip from Salina to Denver, she sat on the floor of the ladies' restroom. Had we known her trip would go like this, we might have been tempted to do what one of the other men did once. He dressed his wife up like a GI and took her on his plane.

Of course, the rest of the trip was crowded, too, but not as bad. Faye and I didn't have to resort to sitting in the bathrooms. Instead, we took turns with other people, sitting six where it was intended for only four to fit.

It was great to be home that year. Our families hadn't seen us since before we were married. Faye and her grandmother had always cut their Christmas tree together, and this year, the two of them cut a second tree, one about three feet tall, for us to take back to Kansas with us. My dad wrapped it in burlap and twine, using a broomstick in the middle to keep it from getting too bent and broken, and we took it on the train with us. It was the hit of the base when we got back to Salina. Very few people had Christmas trees and some of the men made a special trip to come see ours.

In all the hours I spent airborne while stationed in Kansas, there was only one really close call. We were on a high-altitude night formation flight and our crew was in an old, beat up B-17. It had just been to a civilian repair depot and someone had used a fuel line where a high-pressure oil line should have gone, and when we reached altitude, it ruptured. The oil pressure gauge started streaking down. We hit the button to feather the prop, which would have turned the blades in to minimize drag. But with no oil, the prop governor didn't work, and the prop couldn't be feathered. All we could do was shut the engine down. As luck would have it, the radio wasn't working either. Fighting the drag from the dead, windmilling prop, we dropped out of formation and started looking for a place to set down. We saw lights in the distance, which turned out to be Amarillo, Texas.

We knew that there was a good chance that the windmilling prop would eventually rip free. I did everything I could think of to try to make it so the prop would fall straight down instead of ripping through the side of the plane and into the cockpit. We lowered the flaps and put the landing gear down, trying to create more drag. I even tried going into a stall, hoping that would make it drop off. No luck.

As we got closer to Amarillo, we started hoping, white-knuckled, that the thing would just stay on until we got the plane on the ground. Every second seemed like an eternity.

As we approached the airfield, we could see that the traffic pattern was full of cadet trainers flying a night cross-country. Unable to contact the tower, we started in toward the field, turning our landing lights on and off, hoping that someone down there would notice us in time to give all those cadets a heads-up. Having no way of knowing which runway the tower would assign us, we arbitrarily picked one and horsed the plane down.

The instant the wheels hit the runway, the prop section fell off. The engine had literally melted down. When I went to look at it after we landed, it looked as if someone had taken a cutting torch to it. I could see where the molten metal had dripped along the outside of the engine casing. I felt pretty lucky to be on the ground. By the next morning, the entire front of the engine had dropped onto the hardstand.

Our last ferrying assignment took place just before the group was scheduled to head overseas. General Arnold had granted a ten-day leave to everyone and Colonel Engler had ordered the married men to get everyone home. I had just returned from a long flight and was getting ready to catch up on some much-needed sleep when the phone rang. I was told to report to the field immediately. The field was socked in and a big storm was approaching. Visibility was zero-zero and the field was closed. The squadron operations officer figured we had about thirty minutes to get a planeload of thirty or forty people off the ground toward New York or they would miss their last chance for leave.

It was obvious that the visibility wasn't going to improve, so we decided to do an instrument takeoff. This was a big no-no and both the operations officer and I could have gotten into a lot of trouble. Although it was pretty unconventional, it seemed that I'd done enough takeoffs in B-17s to be able to do them in my sleep. With those wide 10,000-foot-long runways, I felt that as long as we got lined up right, there'd be no problem.

The operations officer ordered a Jeep with a beacon on it to lead us to the end of the runway. It was an eerie experience, but the instruments told us everything we needed to know. We lifted into the fog without incident. At 5000 feet we tuned into the airway beams and set our course. We didn't see the ground until east of Pittsburgh.

Because New York City was a controlled area, a P-51 picked us up as we got close and accompanied us all the way in. We had to spend the night, so Hank Robins, the navigator, Chuck Kazarian, the radio operator, the co-pilot and I got on a subway to Times Square to check out the sights. I'd never been in the city before, and I was amazed at how crowded, dirty, and noisy it was. I really couldn't see the attraction. We went into the Waldorf Astoria to see about getting a room. To our amazement, they gave us the bridal suite and charged us next to nothing. At that time, it seemed that everyone was doing what they could for the war effort. Still, it was always a pleasant surprise when someone gave us special treatment just because of the uniform we wore.

Of course, training at Salina included much more than ferrying planes and people from one place to another. We used B-29s to practice timed takeoffs, bomb runs, and all of the techniques we needed to master to prepare for combat. Due to the recurring technical problems with the early planes, we got lots of practice with mechanical failures. During my time at Salina, I personally experienced eleven engine failures, including the one on the B-17. There were lots of problems keeping the engines cool and they tended to catch fire. With four engines, however, the loss of a single engine wasn't much cause for alarm. You just feathered the prop and shut the engine down.

Naturally, if both engines failed on a wing, you had a problem, especially if it happened on takeoff. That might be what happened to a B-29 at Salina. On this particular day, we were rolling through the takeoffs like clockwork. We were supposed to be rolling through them quickly, one plane after another. I pulled into position at the end of the runway just in time to see the plane in front of me lift off, turn toward the city of Salina, stall, and crash. An enormous fireball rose to the sky immediately. It was clear that all on board were dead.

As I tried to recover my breath and collect my thoughts, I heard the tower shouting in my ear, "Roll! Take off! Clear the runway!" We took off, peering to our right as plumes of black smoke billowed up from the wreckage. The plane wasn't from our squadron, so I didn't know the men, but it still shook me up. The Army brought in several high-ranking officers to investigate the cause of the crash. Later, as an eyewitness, I was called to testify about what I had seen. I remembered noticing that as I had pulled into position, one of the props on the plane ahead of me didn't seem to be turning up to speed and the plane didn't seem to be rolling very fast. It is my belief that as they lifted, they intended to feather the problem engine and feathered the prop on the second engine on the wing instead.

Witnessing that crash and having to roll anyway, was a powerful lesson about what piloting a B-29 was all about.

Getting the job done.

Circling the Globe

"They shall mount up with wings like eagles; they shall run and not be weary; and they shall walk and not faint."

Isaiah 40:31

As the spring of 1944 approached, the group began to gear up for heading overseas and beginning our assault on the Japanese homeland. We would launch our missions from advance bases in China, but we would be stationed and barracked in India. At the beginning, only half of the crews would have planes, alternating missions with another crew to keep the planes in the air as much as possible.

There hadn't been many changes in crew assignments up to that point, so I was surprised one day when the operations officer called me into his office and asked if I would be willing to switch co-pilots with another crew. Apparently, the pilot and co-pilot were having trouble getting along and they wanted to find a crew where the co-pilot might work out a little better. I hated to give up Tolzmann; he was not only a fine co-pilot, but a friend, too. Still, I felt that if the Army needed me to switch, it was my duty to agree. I also figured that I could get along with anybody.

Our new co-pilot was named Bill Rewitz. He was married and had a baby. He had come into the program from B-17 transition school. Because co-pilots didn't normally do much actual flying, I took him out in a B-29 and had him shoot some landings, just to reassure myself that he could do it if needed. Although

Rewitz always kept pretty much to himself, he did his job and didn't cause us any problems. We continued our preparations for heading overseas.

Due to the chronic engine problems we experienced with B-29s, the group was under standing orders to replace engines whenever they got two hundred hours on them. As a precaution for the long flight overseas, we were ordered to replace all of the engines on all of the planes. Because the planes and flight crews would arrive in India well ahead of the maintenance crews, who would be going by sea, the flight crews were ordered to change the engines. We would need to change them again in India before the ground crews arrived.

It was still winter in Kansas, twenty below zero and the wind howling, and of course, the planes were all parked out in the weather on hardstands. Everything was covered with ice. We all donned our fleece-lined flight suits and with the crew chief, who was in charge of the ground crew, to direct and coach us, erected canvas blinds to serve as windbreaks around the planes. Still, it was bitter cold. We had big diesel-powered heaters inside the blinds going nonstop. At most, we could only work for a few minutes before stopping to thaw our numb hands in front of the heaters. This went on for days, and the work was truly miserable. Our only comfort came from knowing that the next time we changed engines, we could expect the weather to be a lot warmer.

Because there weren't enough planes, some of the flight crews shipped out early with the ground support personnel, the majority of the spare parts, and supplies. The crew chiefs were left behind to help maintain the planes and fly over with the flight crews. Those of us who did not go by sea would fly the planes over in a multi-legged mission that would take us to the other side of the globe. The departure of half the crews and the ground personnel made it all seem real. We really were going. And soon.

One crew from each squadron was notified that it would be left behind to check out the crews who would be coming in for training after us. As had happened in Tucson, I was going to be left behind. Only this time, my crew stayed with me. Early in March, we watched as dozens of B-29s filled the sky on their way overseas. Because this would be the first time the new planes would be seen by the enemy, the first crews went via Newfoundland in an attempt to convince the Japanese that the B-29s were headed for the European Theater. The remaining crews headed toward South America and then Africa on the way to India.

It was hard to say goodbye to all the men we'd come to know so well. Based on my Tucson experience, I figured I'd never see the 468th again.

Once the squadron left, those of us who remained behind had six weeks to kill with no real duties to perform before the next group arrived. Still, we were required to report to the base each morning. We played a lot of pool at the Officer's Club, often taking our wives with us. Most of the time, we just checked in and went home. Because Al had shipped out, and Sirrka had moved back to Massachusetts, Roberts and his wife, Betty, moved into our apartment with us. We spent hours at the kitchen table laughing over Pinochle, men against the women. It was a pretty even pairing, so there was lots of teasing and competitive kidding about the card games. We had a rule that the losers had to do the dishes. Needless to say, Roberts and I spent some time at the sink.

Because our tail gunner, Sam Nixon, was from Salina, these six weeks were especially nice for him and his family. I couldn't give him leave, but he was grateful for all the passes home that I could write.

Finally, we were sent to pick up our plane from the factory in Wichita. It was an exciting day for all of us. The entire crew went. Part of taking delivery of the plane was that I had to go to the factory office and sign the voucher on behalf of the Army. It was made out for over a million dollars. That alone would have made it a momentous day for me.

Our plane was beautiful, enormous, gleaming silver, and we all fell in love with her. It was obvious that she would need a name other than the aircraft number, 42-6408, assigned at the factory, and we began to discuss the issue.

I had a very clear idea of what I thought we should call her. And even though Colonel Engler had issued clear orders that there would be no nose art on any planes in the 468th, I also had a clear idea of how she should look. The squadron was halfway around the world and I didn't really expect to get to join them. I made a decision, as pilot, that we would not only christen the plane, but paint her as well.

I knew exactly which picture I wanted to use. It was a stunning red-haired Varga Girl, sitting on a rug and turned slightly away, looking back over her shoulder. I thought of her as sitting on a flying carpet. The plane would be named Reddy Teddy. Some of the boys on the crew were deeply religious and objected strongly to my proposal. While I didn't swear, didn't drink much or smoke, and considered myself a moral person, I knew our plane needed to have a name and image with some real 'oomph' to it. I persisted. I was the boss.

We paid a man on base twenty-five dollars to paint the nose during his off-hours. I'd seen his work on a number of other planes, and knew he was the man for the job. I don't recall his name. He was a sergeant in the M.P.s, an African-American, and an extremely gifted painter. The Reddy Teddy was flawless.

Eventually, the next group arrived, and we started making check flights. This included checking out the incoming group commander, Colonel Cheesley. Colonel Cheesley had been Chief Pilot at Delta Airlines before the war, and he told me that if I made it through

Nose art on the Reddy Teddy.

the war, to be sure to look him up and he'd give me a job. I believed him to be sincere, and thought there would be nothing more fun than being a commercial pilot. Maybe being left behind had worked out okay.

As soon as we'd worked our way through the group, we were issued orders to rejoin our squadron. We'd be flying alone on our long journey to India, relying on our own navigation, with very few places to set down should trouble arise. Fortunately, we had a crack navigator, Robins. Although much of a B-29 was extremely high-tech, navigation was a mixture of the very old and the very new. When flying at night, Robins used celestial navigation, sighting his sextant through a Plexiglas bubble. He had always been right on the money. Our arrival times were always within a few minutes of his estimates, and would be, even on our long flights around the globe.

We left on June 4, 1944, two days before D-Day. Our plane was loaded beyond capacity. The bomb bays were filled with fuel tanks and large wooden platforms piled high with spare parts. We were also carrying a spare engine. As soon as we took off, I headed toward Salina. Faye, Betty Roberts, Robins' wife, and Kennard's wife were waiting in the backyard of the house where our apartment was located. They waved as we flew over at five hundred feet or so (another big no-no) and I waggled the wings in salute.

While I was sad to leave Faye, I was also excited. I was embarking on a thrilling adventure, one for which I had been preparing for two years. I was pilot of one of the most advanced planes in the world and was about to fly it across parts of four continents. I was, at last, going to help end the war in the Pacific.

The trip was plotted out in eight-to-ten-hour legs all the way to India. We had fixed orders on where we would land and stay each night. Our first stop was Miami. We had to tinker on the plane a bit that night, which was not at all uncommon for B-29s, so we didn't leave the base. The next day we flew over water and the northeast coast of South America to British Guiana. We were going to spend the night and refuel at a little place named New Georgetown.

You'd think that with all those hours in the air, the crew would have plenty of time to talk. In reality, flying a B-29 was pretty much a full-time job for all concerned. Everyone, except the gunners, had plenty of work to do, and had to stay on task. We really didn't have time for idle chatter. Plus, each person was fairly isolated. For example, Kennard, our flight engineer, sat well behind us facing panels of controls and gauges. He was constantly busy keeping the fuel tanks balanced and the other systems operating correctly. He couldn't possibly have participated in much conversation. Also, even though the plane was pressurized, it was still incredibly noisy. It was difficult to communicate much beyond the bare essentials. And so, long flights were a time of working in some isolation. We were alone with our thoughts and, while in some ways, the flight to India was a fascinating shared experience, in other ways, it was a trip we each made alone.

For me, the flight to British Guiana consisted of hours of monotony punctuated by periods of interest. We had maintained an altitude of 10,000 feet the entire way to conserve fuel and to keep above any possible interfering traffic. There isn't much to see flying for hours over the ocean, and after the initial impressions of novelty, the land eventually became as monotonous as the sea had been. The jungle looked like a vast green lawn that stretched endlessly to the horizon. I was astounded at the enormity of it. And

Airborne B-29 Superfortresses.

while there was a sameness to it, I was excited to be somewhere so foreign and unfamiliar. This new exotic terrain was a signal that we really were on our way. Even through my concentration on the details of flight, and the boredom of the unvarying landscape, the sense of adventure was thrilling. I was excited to be there and was enveloped by a sense of anticipation.

When we first spotted the airstrip, it looked like a tiny bare spot scratched into a carpet. As we began our descent, the carpet began to transform into towering trees and lush jungle greenery.

The airstrip looked impossibly small. Had it not been for our orders to land there, I would have been tempted to bypass it, thinking we'd never get out of there again even if we did manage to touch down and stop safely. The closer we got, the smaller it looked. The jungle vegetation grew right up to the edge of the strip and, at the end of the runway, positioned like massive pillars, were several trees that I assumed to be palms.

I knew that runway was too short; it wasn't half as long as the strips we'd used at home. As we came in on our approach, I could hear Rewitz repeating, "Watch those trees. Watch those trees." I'd never cut power faster or stood on the brakes as hard. The palms looked even bigger from the runway as we hurtled toward them, brakes squealing. Miraculously, we stopped just short of the end of the runway, our vision filled with the enormous tree trunks just beyond our nose. Rewitz and I took a deep breath, looked at each other, and then began our taxi to the hardstand.

We were surrounded by jungle, huge towering walls of green on all sides. As we dropped out of the plane, one by one, our senses were flooded with the noise of thousands of birds and animals calling and screeching. We were unaccustomed to the hot steamy air and found it heavy and hard to breathe. Looking around us, it seemed as if we had fallen into another world; one from which, impossibly, the only exit was straight up.

Our assigned quarters for the night were thatched-roof structures built on tall stilts to discourage snakes and other animals from finding their way in. We climbed the steps, sweating, hot, and tired, and found our cots—each equipped with mosquito netting. We didn't leave the base that night—there was no place to go—but Kennard did manage to buy a souvenir.

I found out about it the next morning while we were loading the plane. He had paid twenty dollars for a small monkey, which he intended to take with us to India. I wasn't thrilled with the idea, and in fact thought it a rather poor one. I laid down the law that the monkey would be nowhere near the controls of the aircraft. Kennard would have to put it, and the stalk of bananas he had bought with it, in the rear pressure cabin and ask the rest of the crew to watch after it.

But having the monkey on board was not my biggest worry that morning. I kept looking at that short runway. I had no idea how we were going to get off the ground.

When it came time to leave, we taxied to the extreme end of the runway and squared around, extending the rear of the plane above unpaved field, giving us every possible foot of pavement. At that point, there was only one thing to do: make it work. I held the brakes until I had the throttle open to two-thirds. As we started to roll, I gave it everything I could, full throttle. On one hand, it seemed as if we were creeping along. On the other, we were devouring runway at an alarming rate. When I felt we could wait no longer, I lifted the nose and we started to rise. Grinding, groaning, the engines pulled as we lifted in a steep climb.

By the time we were out of runway and began to skim over the trees, we were so close to the tops of them, we could have counted the leaves. We'd made it.

As heavily loaded as we were, we couldn't climb steeply for more than a few seconds without stalling, so we had to back off as soon as we cleared the trees. We eventually reached altitude and leveled off to cruise for what seemed to me an uneventful flight over more jungle to Natal, Brazil.

Little did we know in the forward pressure cabin that Kennard's monkey and the men in the rear were having a very eventful time. The monkey had gone berserk when the plane took off, and someone had been feeding it bananas, trying to keep it calm. Unfortunately, they were having little success. The monkey was running absolutely wild. It was doing loop-the-loops around the inside of the plane, running up one side, across the ceiling and down the other. Due to stress, or the bananas, or a combination of both, it had developed a severe case of diarrhea, and was leaving a smelly messy trail as it caromed around the plane.

When we landed in Brazil and I heard about the mess, I peeked my head into rear pressure cabin. I was furious. Kennard was on clean-up duty for hours.

It was dusk when we landed in Brazil, and it soon became dark, so we weren't able to see much of the area around Natal, but we had flown over the Amazon River, near the mouth, where it had spread into a broad delta, sixty miles wide. Thankfully, because it was late evening, it wasn't as hot in Natal as it had been in Georgetown. It was here that I bought some beautiful boots for myself. They were actually riding boots, probably about eight inches high from heel to top, but everyone called them mosquito boots. I loved them because the cuffs of my uniform trousers fit over the tops. While they weren't regulation, most flyers who came through bought them, and the PX was full of them. I also bought souvenirs to mail home for Faye and my mom. I bought Faye some silk hose, which were impossible to buy in the States during the war, and I bought alligator handbags for both my mother and Faye.

From Natal, we headed out across ocean, roughly toward Ascension Island, our halfway point to Africa. By the time we reached the vicinity of Ascension, it was getting dark. It was going to be a long night as we flew toward Africa and the Gold Coast.

As we neared the bulge of Africa, we dropped down to about five hundred feet to take advantage of the strong westerly winds. We landed at Accra the next morning, battling strong tail winds. Our orders were to fly over land only at night the rest of the way, so we had the day free to rest. We didn't leave the base, but again, I went shopping for Faye at the PX and bought a delicate gold bracelet decorated with tiny elephants. As I mailed it, I thought of her, by now on her way back home to Oregon. I liked to think of her surprise as she opened the packages I'd sent. I imagined going somewhere with her when I got home and her wearing the bracelet.

That night we crossed Africa, heading to Khartoum, in the Egyptian Sudan. There, we were assigned to a barracks and decided to take a walk along the Nile. We went as a group. Except for near the river, where there were a few palm trees and it was irrigated, the terrain was arid and sandy. The banks of the river were flat and open, and we could see a long way both up and down the river. There was a lot of traffic on the water, and we enjoyed watching the variety of ships, especially the boats with the large brightly-colored striped sails, moving up and down the river.

I was intrigued by the ancient irrigation system we saw in place. Because there was no metal or wood available in the area, the water was moved in woven baskets which were suspended on ropes made of what I assumed to be grape vines. There was a turntable of sorts to which a shoddy-looking cow was yoked. A man poked the cow with a stick, the cow trudged around the turntable, and the whole apparatus creaked into motion, as basket-by-basket, river water was transferred into the irrigation ditch.

Unfortunately, our plans to leave the next evening had to be changed due to a severe dust storm, or *habub* (pronounced ha-bōōb'), that blew into the area. We were stranded at Khartoum for two or three days, unable to leave the barracks. Much worse than fog, the visibility was zero, and the sheets of sand and dust hurled by high winds made breathing outdoors almost impossible. As we looked out the window, only blowing blankets of dust were visible. We could see no trace of the buildings just across the street.

Despite windows and doors, the dust penetrated everything.

It covered the furniture, our clothing, and got into the food. We put the engine covers on the plane early on, but still, when we took them off, dust was everywhere. We cleaned up what we could, and hoped that the rest would blow out.

Our last night in Khartoum was marred when an M.P. looked me up at an outdoor movie that was showing on base. Kennard had gotten drunk and was in the bathhouse giving everyone a bad time. I followed the M.P. and found Kennard belligerent and staggering. He was on the verge of being placed in the brig. If Kennard was locked up, we'd be without a flight engineer. Who knows how long we would be stranded?

I was furious with him. I racked him to attention and placed him under house arrest. This angered Kennard, and after I was gone, he punched his fist through a window, cutting his hand severely. Somehow, the M.P. managed to wrap some towels around his hand and get him to the base hospital, where they stitched him up. The doctor told us that he really shouldn't fly for a few days, but we were behind schedule for getting to India, and all of us were anxious to get out of Khartoum, so despite Kennard's injury, we prepared to continue our journey the next day. I was certainly grateful to the M.P. for the way he handled the situation.

As we readied the plane that evening, I watched in horror as the ground crew loaded an additional six hundred and forty gallon fuel tank into our bomb bay. At a little over six pounds to the gallon, this was adding two tons to our already heavy plane. "No way," I said. "We're overloaded as it is. We'll never get airborne." Unfortunately, there was no reasoning with the officer in charge. He was convinced that we'd need the extra fuel to get to India. I knew otherwise. I showed him the cruise control and gross weight charts. I cited the long flight from South America. Orders were orders, however. He outranked me, and he just wouldn't budge.

I checked and rechecked the conditions. It had been a hot day.

The sensitive engines were going to heat up faster and the lift was going to be severely hampered by the atmospheric conditions.

"The engines are going to burn up on takeoff," I stated flatly.

The man was made of steel. I was flying that plane out of there, load intact, or else. Seeing that I couldn't lighten the load, I lobbied for taking off early the next morning, say at five A.M. It would be cooler then and we'd at least have a chance of getting airborne. It wasn't an option.

Finally, I struck a bargain with him. I'd only try it if they would tow the plane to the end of the runway so I didn't have to idle long in the heat before we rolled.

The tow vehicle groaned as the plane slowly began to inch forward. I called for temperature readings, wind speed and direction over and over, praying for a drop in degree or a boost in velocity. Every bump felt like the thud of dead weight.

In my mind, I spoke affectionately to the plane, "Come on, Teddy. Get us out of here."

I was in a cold white sweat as we lined up at the end of the runway. It didn't look long or short to me, only hopeless. I listened closely to each engine as it roared to life. Not a miss or hitch. I skipped the normal end-of-the-runway runup on the checklist which called for taking it to full throttle and two thousand rpms. I figured it was better to trust the engines and keep them cooler than to do the runup and increase the chances of engine failure.

I closed my eyes and envisioned us taking off. I saw us speeding down the runway, gaining momentum. I imagined us clearing the end of the runway and gaining elevation. Every sense was on alert. I was keenly aware of the feel of the wheel in my hand, the sound of the engines, and every detail of the runway ahead.

We rolled. Full throttle.

Nothing more than a gentle lumbering.

We crawled along the runway. I could feel no lift under the

wings at all. There was nothing. She was dead weight on wheels. Slowly, slowly, we got going a little faster. Still nothing.

Too soon, we were out of runway. No room to stop, and only hints of lift. There was nothing to do but pull the nose up and pray. There was a wire fence dead ahead. Almost in disbelief, I watched it glide under us. Fortunately, there were no more obstacles to clear, and the desert was flat. We were only about twenty feet off the ground, and there was no evidence that we would go any higher.

We flew in white-knuckled silence, expecting to drop like lead any instant. With all the fuel we had on board, the fireball would have been enormous. Although we were going in the wrong direction, I didn't dare try to turn. I just kept the plane headed straight out from the strip, hoping to play on any signs of lift. There simply were none.

Before long, we saw a native village dead ahead. I didn't dare try to turn. There were no tall buildings, just huts, so I stayed the course. We were still at only about twenty feet elevation, and we could see the people scattering as we approached, but we cleared the huts and continued. While the terrain was mostly flat grasslands, there were some little hillocks that rose up in gentle mounds. I found myself steering around small rises that I wouldn't even have noticed under normal circumstances.

The engines groaned on relentlessly. All four were way past the red zone, and we'd gone miles with no gain in altitude. Kennard worked frantically, doing everything he could to take the load off the engines, but there wasn't much he could do. If we cut back at all, we'd stall. If we raised flaps, we'd be goners. How long would these sensitive engines hold? To say we were scared silly would be an understatement.

Eventually, though, as we burned some of the fuel and the load began to lighten, the engines started to cool, and we slowly gained altitude. We ground our way into the sky, devouring boatloads of fuel in defiance of all the rules of gravity and engineering.

It had been awhile since we left the base, and we hadn't checked in. It was now time to turn and get back on course. We flew straight over the base and made our required transmission as we headed out. "All normal," we reported.

That night, we flew to Karachi, which is now in Pakistan but was then in India. We were not allowed to fly over Saudi Arabia, so when we reached it, we flew down the west side of it, along the Red Sea, around the end of the peninsula, over the Gulf of Aden and then across the Arabian Sea. As we approached Karachi in the morning, we were ordered into a holding pattern at a thousand feet due to heavy traffic. The base was close to the city. The terrain was more hilly than what we'd left in Khartoum, and in the morning light, everything looked brown. The buildings, the ground, all seemed made of the same dusty material.

Even with the concentration required as we flew the pattern and long approach, and the fact that we were all tired and hungry, we became aware of a smell in the forward pressure cabin. We started looking around and commenting as it grew steadily stronger. "What's going on?" we asked each other. It smelled like an open sewer. Nothing inside the plane accounted for the smell, which soon grew to nauseating proportions. Finally, we radioed the tower, asking if it could be coming from the ground. Smell confirmed. It was the city itself.

After we landed and had parked in the hardstand, one of the ground crew reported that we'd brought along a little souvenir. We looked to where he was pointing at the rear of the plane. Hanging on the tail skid was a hundred feet of that fence I'd thought we cleared in Khartoum.

It was exciting to have only one more leg to fly to be reunited with our Group. We eagerly left Karachi the next morning for what was to be our home base in Kharagpur, about one hundred miles outside Calcutta. As we approached Kharagpur, almost giddy at being at the end of our long solo journey, we called for landing instructions and were told that the runway was closed. A transport plane from the Air Transport Command had crashed on it and we had to be diverted to an ATC strip a few miles away to wait for the runway to be cleared. When we landed at the other base, disappointed and hungry, an officer came out to meet us. Our disappointment didn't seem to begin to match his displeasure at seeing us. The contrast between the smiling faces and warm handshakes we had expected in Kharagpur and this man's cold, glum demeanor couldn't have been more dramatic.

"Say," I said to him, "we haven't eaten since breakfast. Is there somewhere we could grab a bite to eat while we wait?" He pointed to a low wooden building nearby and said, "That's the mess hall, but only personnel from the base are allowed in. You'll just have to wait until you get to where you're going. In fact, you'd better just stay with your plane."

We were accustomed to leaving crew personnel or guards with the plane, but this time we had no choice but for all of us to sit and wait with the plane. We sat for hours waiting for the go-ahead.

I guess that should have prepared us for disappointing greetings. When we finally landed at Kharagpur later that evening, Lt. Colonel Edmundson and Colonel Engler came out in a Jeep to meet the plane. It was great to see Colonel Jim again. He seemed genuinely pleased to see us and was anxious to get details about the trip and the performance of the plane. Colonel Engler said only one thing as he glared at Teddy painted on the nose. "That picture will come off in the morning."

As it turned out, Colonel Jim must have gone to bat for us with Engler. The next morning he looked me up and told me the picture could stay. For the entire time I was in India, we had the only painted plane in the squadron.

The base at Karaghpur was owned by the British and had been there some time before the war started. Karaghpur was hot, arid and flat, and the food in the officers' mess was terrible. The Army used native cooks who tried to make American food, but never seemed to get it right. The main course seemed to always be Spam. The barracks were long low buildings with steeply sloping roofs and long open porches supported by poles dug into the ground. The ceilings were open, and looking up, you could see the framework of two-foot-thick split bamboo that supported the thatch laid on top. The roofs were infested with thousands of termites that caused a continual rain of sawdust to fall inside the barracks. The white sawdust coated everything, and if you left your shoes on the dirt floor, the termites would eat the soles off. For this reason, we had to stow our shoes either inside our foot lockers or on the beds. The termites weren't the only troublesome insects. Each bunk was covered with a mosquito net.

There were also snakes. The first cobra I saw was at the barracks. Several of us were sitting on the porch in armchairs when one crawled out into the dirt just in front of us. It raised up in the dust and looked around. One of the men calmly stood up, went inside and got his .45, and shot it. That was that.

There wasn't much difference between the officers' quarters and the enlisted men's barracks. Both were somewhat primitive, but one thing that eased things substantially for the officers, was that each of us had a bearer, or personal servant. The job of the bearer was to attend to the barracks and guard your belongings. He washed your clothing in the river, and somehow pressed it. Each barracks had a Lister Bag, which was a canvas water bag that the bearer kept filled and treated with chlorine. The theory behind the Lister Bag was that the condensation that accumulated on the outside of the bag kept the water inside cooler. During the day, the bearer kept the bag in the shade, moving it whenever necessary. The water tasted terrible, but at least you could drink it with some degree of safety.

I paid my bearer twelve dollars a month. Mine was only twelve years old, but at the base, he was making more money than his father was, who worked in town. As a bonus once, I gave him a black umbrella, which was considered a mark of distinction. He was delighted with the gift and carried it proudly.

Naturally, one of the first things I did when we arrived was to look up my buddies from Kansas. It was strange to suddenly be in a place as foreign as India, but at the same time be surrounded by so many familiar faces. In the weeks since the group had arrived, they had already flown a few missions. Suddenly, the reality of war sank in. Pattillo, Brown, and Reida were all there. But my good, good friend, Ivanovich, and his co-pilot Connie McMichael were gone. They had died in a night raid over Yawata before I'd even arrived.

How could the rest of the gang be there without Ivanovich showing up at any moment? Somehow, though, the machinery of war didn't pause for adjustments to things like the death of a friend. The group was gearing up for its next raid over Anshan, in Manchuria, and our crew and the Reddy Teddy were put to work immediately.

The Hump

"The Hump was aptly named. Between embattled China and the Allied supply bases in India, there rose the 20,000-foot—and then some—Himalayas, the most awesome mountain ranges on our planet. There were no emergency landing fields below, only the desolation of rocky slopes, glaciers and ice-covered peaks. To abandon a crippled plane and bail out was only to court a lingering death in the endless mountains or trackless Burmese jungle, beyond. ...a thousand airmen...lost their lives flying the Hump.

Lowell Thomas, *So Long Until Tomorrow: From Quaker Hill to Kathmandu*

To mount a mission over the Japanese homeland was a Herculean task in those first days of the B-29's deployment. The Japanese were already occupying much of the interior of China and most of the Pacific. It was too risky to base operations in western China, because they would be within striking distance of the Japanese forces, but it was impossible to reach Japan directly from India or from any other Allied territories. The only option was to establish advance bases in China, and use them intermittently as staging points for missions originating in India.

To prepare for a mission, each squadron had to ferry all the necessary supplies from India to its base in China. This included hundreds of thousands of gallons of fuel, spare parts, bombs and ammunition, and much of the food to feed several hundred men. Because it took the entire squadron and every available plane several trips between India and China to stock the forward base, supplies had to be flown in, not only for the bombing mission, but for the many ferrying missions as well.

"The Hump," as the Himalayas were known to us, were more than a mountain range. They were a formidable wall that loomed in defiance of any attempt to master it. Flying this route was unlike anything I'd ever experienced. Violent weather could materialize in an instant, throwing wind, lightning, and slashing, driving snow against us at full force. Visibility was usually nonexistent, and it was easy to get off course and get lost. Even on good days, the altitude requirements were unforgiving. We seldom flew below 21,000 feet, and usually were at 26,000. To lose an engine over The Hump in a fully-loaded aircraft could mean doom.

The Army lost so many planes over The Hump that the ferrying runs were soon counted as combat missions. In many ways, flying over the Himalayas felt much riskier than facing anything the Japanese might throw at us.

When we first arrived in India, we still had only one plane per two crews, and another crew was assigned with us to fly Reddy Teddy. Their pilot, Captain Skelley, outranked me and would fly the mission against the big steel mill at Anshan. Meanwhile, we flew old B-17s or B-24s that had been converted to transport planes. On our first ferrying mission, Colonel Jim flew with me, as co-pilot, to check me out. He tried to check out every one of his pilots in this way before they flew The Hump on their own.

We flew a standard route from our India base to China. From Kharagpur, we flew roughly Northeast and up the Assam Valley to Chabua. Naturally, every load to China had to be at capacity, and the planes were always heavy. We began climbing for altitude as soon as we were airborne. Chabua was a check point. If we weren't close to altitude by the time we got there, we weren't going to make it over the mountains and we needed to turn around.

Of the six trips I made to China, we were socked in most of the time. Sometimes, St. Elmo's Fire danced in wavering green lines of static around the engine cowls. Before we had radar installed, we sometimes had to climb as high as 26,000 feet to be sure to clear the highest peaks. Naturally, though, we wanted to stay as low as possible. If you could see the mountains, you could fly lower to save fuel. The goal was to have enough extra fuel for the return trip home from China, that you could pump some of it out and leave it there. We left India with seventy-five hundred gallons of fuel. A bad trip was one where you only left a thousand gallons in China. A really bad trip was one where you had to take on fuel to get home.

After we had been in India a short time, we added the eleventh member to our crew: radar operator, Bob Humphrey. Bob was a tall, lanky kid from Wisconsin, who fit in with the crew right away and did his job well. Bob had been flying with other crews before we arrived, and had bailed out over China due to mechanical failure when hauling fuel for the June 15 mission to Yawata. With his original plane gone, he was available to join our crew.

Some of the first planes that came over from Kansas didn't get radar installed until after they reached India, and as most of the radar operators traveled by sea to India, many didn't have an operator at first even though they had the equipment. Having radar made a big difference in the flights over The Hump. While it no doubt saved lives and planes, it also helped us set a more accurate course. With the help of our radar, our crew was the first to leave two thousand gallons of fuel in China, a real feather in our caps.

We actually saw the mountains on one or two trips. They were a spectacular sight. I was amazed at how close and how rugged they were, even though we were at such high altitude. Huge, jagged rocks loomed up toward us. There was lots of snow, naturally, but there were so many sheer vertical cliffs and rocky outcroppings that the prevailing impression for me was one of stark, massive rock. I could see no sign of vegetation anywhere, and the towering peaks, piled in succession, one after the other on all sides, seemed to go on forever.

Because we wanted to fly as low as possible to save fuel, the flight over the Himalayas was often more of an attempt to fly through them. When we had good visibility, and later with radar, we could fly between the peaks. We could see the rivers plunging down the steep canyons in white foaming torrents. These rivers often meant death to flyers who had to bail out over the mountains. The strong winds, whirling through the peaks and canyons, could suck the parachutes into the raging water where the men were beaten to death against the rocks and boulders. If crewmen were lucky enough to parachute into the Himalayas without serious injury, we were fortunate in that the natives rushed to assist them and served as guides to help them in their return to the base.

One of our crews, with pilot Jim Pattillo, bailed out after losing an engine, and two of the men drowned. The rest of them walked out about a week later. Before the war was over, the crews in the Air Transport Command had many similar tales to tell of "walking out of the Himalayas."

Even when we experienced bad weather "on top," the clouds sometimes cleared as we began to let down on the China side of The Hump. We could often see clearly enough to spot an enormous structure sitting on the top of a big mountain at 12-15,000 feet. At this point, we were flying nearly level with it, and could see the details quite clearly. It looked like a castle, or something out of a storybook, except that it was built on a mammoth scale. It was mind-boggling to consider the task of building such a structure in such a remote and inhospitable location. I never did learn exactly what it was, although I assume it was a monastery of some kind.

While our Hump flights always had some tense moments, there was only one mission which could really be called a close one. We were flying an old war-weary B-24 that had been converted for transport. We were loaded down with food for the base in China. The weather was brutal and two or three planes on the mission had already turned around and gone home. We were determined, though, and pushed on even though there was no visibility and we were being tossed around like a beach ball in surf.

At the top of The Hump, we lost an engine. We were already at the highest point of the trip, and figured we were close to halfway. The rest of the trip would be downhill whether we turned back to India or went on to China, so we pressed on. We feathered the prop immediately and, as we boasted to one another, "delivered the groceries."

After we unloaded the supplies in China, two of our gunners, Dick Bishop and Sam Henry, decided to have a look at the engine. Fortunately, both had spent some time in aircraft mechanic's school before becoming gunners. The engine had nine cylinders and had swallowed a valve. There wasn't a drop of oil in it, but otherwise it seemed okay. Normally, we wouldn't be allowed to fly a plane if it wasn't in good condition before we began a Hump run, and we would have to wait until the next day to get a ride home, but none of us wanted to stay in China overnight. It was an advance base, close to the Japanese lines, and extremely primitive. K-rations were considered a luxury there. Bishop and Henry decided to take the engine apart and reconfigure it to run on the eight good cylinders so we could head home right away. We were all for it.

I went to Colonel Engler, who was at the base, and asked his permission to fly the damaged plane home. He consented, on the condition that if it malfunctioned before the top of The Hump, we'd turn around and come back. The climb out of China was reasonably uneventful, but the engine ran out of oil just as we reached the top. We feathered it and flew on to the base at Chabua on the India side, filled it with oil, then headed home without further incident.

While the logistics of supplying the bases in China were overwhelming, the construction of them was even more so. With the help of the Chinese, the Americans built four advance B-29 bases in China near Chengtu. Each group had its own airfield. The base built for the 468th was known as A-7. When we first flew missions into A-7, it was still under construction. It was usable, but there was a lot more work to be done on it.

The Chinese had no machinery to build the long wide strips the B-29s needed. Every inch of the strip was built by hand. Thousands of laborers worked in swarms around the field. They hauled dirt away in baskets and hauled in gravel that they had crushed with a hammer or made by beating rocks together by hand in a quarry five miles away. Most of them used large woven baskets, but some used two baskets on yokes.

National Archives

Chinese laborers break rocks by hand while building an advance B-29 base in China.

To pave the runways, the Chinese used a concrete or cement roller that was ten feet in diameter. It took two hundred men pulling on long lead lines to move it. As they pulled, they chanted "eeee-haw, eeee-haw," their voices even on the first syllable and falling deep on the second. Pulling the roller was dangerous work. Naturally, it was easier to keep it moving than to get it started, so they tried to keep the momentum going. If the roller got moving too fast, however, the men would break into a sprint before it, trying to get out of the way before it ran over and crushed them. Many died under just these circumstances.

National Archives

Chinese laborers pull a huge cement roller while building B-29 airfields in China.

Another dangerous situation arose out of superstition. Many of the peasants working at the field believed that the props on the engines could chase away any evil spirits that were following them. As soon as a plane touched down and began to taxi, a number of peasants raced onto the airstrip, running ahead of the plane. Their goal was to get as close to the spinning props as possible so the spirits would leave. Obviously, if they misjudged, and were hit, they were chopped into pieces. I had heard accounts from a number of pilots whose planes had been involved in these accidents. It was unnerving to see these people racing ahead of your plane, just inches from death.

We tried everything we could to put a halt to this practice, but the superstition was too strong, and so this became one of the expected hazards of flying into China. Even getting the laborers to clear the field when you wanted to land was problematic. The first time nobody moved on my approach, I thought they must not have heard the plane, so I buzzed the field. They wouldn't move. I eventually learned that all you could do was set the plane down and count on them to get out of the way.

Aside from these difficulties on the field, the Chinese people were warm and friendly. Ever smiling, they met us with the Chinese thumbs up, "*Ding hao,*" wherever we went. There was a little village called Pengshan near the field, with no roads, just foot paths wide enough to accommodate a water buffalo pulling a cart. There were ducks everywhere, thousands of them. They kept the insects down in the rice paddies and were a staple of the villagers' diets. As we walked through the village of split bamboo houses, which were really more like open sheds, we could see row upon row of ducks hanging from the rafters. It seemed that everyone was always carrying buckets of something: water, or rice, or whatever. They also had a barrel factory in the village where they were busily making steel barrels for storing our gasoline at the base.

The Chinese loved American cigarettes. Because we were each issued two cartons a month, I often gave away a pack of cigarettes as a gift. I didn't smoke, and sometimes I gave them to someone on base, but I liked giving them to the Chinese in the village. This was okay with the Army, but if I had sold them, I would have been in trouble. At that time, Camels were going for an appalling twenty dollars per carton on the Chinese black market, yet Army personnel could buy them for sixty cents a carton on base. The Army recognized a potential problem and made it a court-martial offense to sell your cigarettes to the Chinese. I did stretch things a little when I traded some cigarettes for a beautiful hand-embroidered silk bedspread I wanted for Faye. I had already bought her a brocade silk blouse, detailed in intricate gold embroidery, from one of the villagers. Silk was so scarce in the United States during the war due to the Army's insatiable demand for silk parachutes, that women hoarded their silk stockings like fine jewelry. I smiled to think of bringing Faye yards and yards of the precious material.

In addition to the cigarettes, we were issued two cases of canned fruit juice, and the officers also got two fifths of whiskey each month. I seldom drank, and had a strict rule about drinking alcohol if I expected to fly within the following twenty-four hours. This made the whiskey fairly worthless to me, so I often traded mine to the enlisted men for their fruit juice.

There were rice paddies and canals right up to the edge of the airfield. The quiet canals were equipped with tall wooden water wheels that the Chinese used to pump water into the paddies. The wheels were equipped with a series of wooden buckets, much along the idea of a Ferris Wheel at a carnival, except the buckets were set at a fixed angle. On each side of the wheel were long spokes radiating out from the hub. It reminded me of the wheel on a sailing vessel. At the end of each long spoke was a little flattened area. To operate the wheel, a man on each side stepped up from the supporting frame and onto the end of a spoke, and then merely started stepping on the spokes as they came along. The men's weight and their leg-power against the lever-spokes converted into the tremendous power needed to turn the hub. Once it started turning, the buckets at the bottom of the wheel scooped up the water, and then as they came over the top, the same angle that made them scoop water from below, made the water dump out as the buckets came down the back of the wheel. It was an ingenious device, and I watched with fascination as the water levels changed.

On the rare occasions when we had to stay overnight at A-7, we were usually fed water buffalo, lots of rice, and coffee or tea. The coffee and tea were extremely bitter. I think both beverages were boiled in the same pot, because they tasted the same. The water buffalo was unbelievably tough to chew, but we knew we were faring better than the men on the line (ground crews) who were stationed there. To them, the K-rations we hauled over The Hump were a treat. While they complained about the food, I think some of them simply preferred to relax and settle for K-rations in the barracks than make the long hike down to the Chinese mess.

The bathing facilities were also primitive. To take a shower, you went to the bath house. There was usually a Chinese worker there who kept a fire burning under a large square wooden tub that had a metal bottom. When you went in, the worker would dip a bucketful of the hot water for you. You then attached the bucket to a pulley apparatus. There were holes in the bottom of the tub that you opened by pulling on a line attached to a float inside the bucket. To get wet, you just hoisted the bucket up with the pulleys and tugged on the line. Once you were a little wet, you let go of the line, soaped up, and then hoped you'd left enough water in the bucket to rinse. It was always a gamble whether that second pull of the line would leave you rinsed or soapy. A-7 was an incredibly dusty place, even though it was in such a mountainous area, so even this little bit of washing felt good.

The dust at A-7 caused more than discomfort, though. The big open fields were so large, and it was so dusty with the big planes landing and taking off, that the Army sprayed tung oil over the airstrips, taxiways, and hardstands to keep the dust down and the bases functional. The Chinese supplied the tung oil as part of their agreement with the Army, and it was extremely expensive, but because there was so much dust, we used a lot of it. The problem with it though, was that it covered the planes with a thin, sticky oily film that caused trouble with lift. For planes loaded for a long-range mission, it was sometimes a critical factor. We used gasoline as a solvent to get rid of the oil, and I was constantly after the crew to wash down the plane.

I was a stickler for keeping the planes—especially the Reddy Teddy—shipshape, even without the tung oil problem, and I guess that after awhile I developed a characteristic way of issuing the order to wash them. One day, I happened to jump out of the cockpit just in time to hear young Humphrey say to the crew, in what I thought was an extremely unflattering imitation of me, "Let's get this plane washed down, boys."

You could almost hear their smiles shatter as they caught sight of me glowering up behind them.

What I would have given in the months to follow to have them all alive and able to make fun of me again.

The Mission

"He fell in October 1918, on a day which was so peaceful and quiet on the whole front, the Army bulletin confined itself to a single line: In the West there is nothing new to report."

Erich Maria Remarque
All Quiet on the Western Front

When Captain Skelley and his crew returned from the Anshan mission with the Reddy Teddy intact, I knew that our crew was in line to participate in the next mission. After all the years of preparation and delay, I was finally going to fly into combat. The prospect was exciting to me. I was really going to help get the job done against what I felt to be an almost inhuman and evil enemy. Flying a mission would be both an adventure and an accomplishment. At 26, I still had all the invincibility of youth. I wasn't afraid or anxious that something might happen to us on a mission. After all, we were flying the fastest, biggest, most accurate bomber in the world. No plane was more advanced. Who could touch us? If someone came after us, we'd just shoot him down.

While I knew that the Army could expect to suffer losses in every mission, it never crossed my mind that it was us who could be shot down or injured. We'd been in many touchy situations in the past and had always come through unscathed. Certainly, being shot down was something that happened to other people. Not to me, and not to my crew. I looked forward to the mission, not with dread, but with anticipation. The ferrying missions to China continued, this time in preparation for "our mission." It would be nearly a month before our turn came. The time passed slowly for me despite the flights over The Hump and the maintenance work on the Reddy Teddy. Still, there were a few incidents to break the monotony.

We were still changing the temperamental engines frequently and one day found that the base didn't have a part we needed. I was told we could pick it up at a field eighty miles away. We had a little single-engine L-5 at the base for evacuating wounded and running short errands. I'd never seen an L-5 before, but my heart leapt at the chance to fly one. I was like a teenager being handed the keys to the car and asked to drive to the store for milk. The idea of checking myself out in a new plane didn't faze me a bit, and I doubt any of the other pilots would have thought anything of it, either. I just walked up to the plane, saw that it had gas in it, climbed in, and fired it up. There was no radio in the plane, so I watched the tower and waited until they flashed me a green light.

As was standard procedure in a new plane, the first thing I did when safely airborne was to take it into a stall. This let me know how the plane would feel coming in for a landing. I did that, and with no maps or navigational aids, I "just followed the railroad tracks" as I had been told to do, and landed when I got to an airfield. I had the needed part in minutes, climbed back into my little plane, which I was wishing I owned, and returned to base.

We also took leave during this waiting period. We usually went into Kharagpur, but one time the whole crew decided to take the train to Calcutta. I was struck by how crowded India was and how poor so many people seemed to be. We jammed into trains where every square inch of space was taken up by bodies. We pressed together with hardly room to breathe. Those who couldn't fit inside the train grabbed onto the outside, joining the mob that hung from the sides.

The streets in Calcutta were narrow, crowded and noisy. Children ran about, dirty, nearly naked, and seemingly abandoned. Lepers and the blind or crippled crouched along the walls begging for money. Human waste ran in channels dug into the street and eventually emptied into the Ganges River, which appeared to be just a larger running sewer. The smell was overwhelming. Walking through the hot muggy streets made me realize how precious America was. Even as poor as I had been as a child, I had experienced nothing compared to this.

We decided to stay at the New Grande Hotel, which was designated as a hotel for officers only. It was a fancy place, quite English in style. We wanted to keep the group together and decided that we should all stay there, officers and enlisted men alike. Two of us went in and booked the rooms. Then the officers of the group went in and, bit by bit, we all brought pieces of our extra clothing out to the rest of the men and swapped them for some of their stuff. With the whole crew dressed as officers, we strode in and out of the hotel at will. Had the staff looked closely, though, they'd have seen a little non-officer attire on each one of us. We had a great time there. The food was served in several courses, and it was all magnificent.

Naturally, we saw the tourist sights and bought some souvenirs, but it was hard for me to take them in and truly appreciate them. What I had seen on the train and in the streets left a much stronger impression. I took several pictures in India, but it was not an exotic or fascinating place to me. It was only tragic.

Finally the day arrived for the last ferrying mission to China in preparation for our first combat mission. We had installed our new engines, and Teddy was ready to go. Instead of the gasoline and supplies we usually took, this time our bomb bays were loaded with unarmed bombs. Some of the fellas used chalk and wrote on some of them, "This is for Ivanovich," and, "For Ivanovich."

We flew the Reddy Teddy over The Hump, knowing that we would be spending the night at A-7 in preparation for an early takeoff the next morning. I knew there were a certain number of missions to fly in a tour of duty. At this time, it was fifty. Later, it would be changed to thirty-five. This first real combat mission would be just one of many notches on the wall. I looked forward to watching the number grow and was curious about what the particulars would be behind each one.

That evening at A-7, Rewitz, my co-pilot; Robins, the navigator; and Roberts, the bombardier; and I went to the briefings. The room was crowded, filled with young men who knew that the success of the mission and their chances of getting back depended in large part on how well they absorbed the information they would be given that night. All were careful to take notes and double-check the maps and reconnaissance photos. The same preparations were being made at other advance bases throughout the region.

We were launching a massive attack on the largest steel mill in Japan, the Imperial Iron and Steel Works at Yawata, on the southern-most island of Kyushu. Wave after wave of B-29s would fill the skies in the morning and knock out part of Japan's ability to wage war. It would be the first daylight B-29 raid over Japan. There had already been a mission over Yawata (6/15/44) that had not been as effective as anticipated, so the Army decided to mount cameras in the bomb bays to record additional information about the site and to better evaluate our methods. Therefore, instead of peeling off right after the bombs were released, we were to continue to fly straight and level for a full minute after bombs away. No evasive maneuvers, no flying up and out of flak or fighter attack. This meant a two-minute bomb run, an interminable length of time to be so exposed and so vulnerable, considering that a normal bomb run was thirty to forty-five seconds.

As we left the briefing, I looked at my three crew members.

The mission was a tough one. While daylight raids were more risky, the hope was that if the weather cooperated, the better visibility of daytime would increase bombing accuracy. The vulnerability of the one full minute of photography after bombs away underscored the importance of being sure the target was destroyed. The Army did not want us to have to go back again and they were upping the stakes to be sure the job was done.

Because we had to take so much fuel with us, we could only carry six, five-hundred pound bombs to Yawata. Our crew had participated in the massive preparations made to launch this mission. We knew how much was invested in money, resources, time, and in lives, just to give us the opportunity to get those six bombs over the target. Every bomb had to count. If any of the guys felt afraid of dying or getting hurt, it didn't show. Instead, I believe that we mostly felt the tremendous weight of the responsibility we had been handed. To succeed was the only option. To fail was unthinkable.

A familiar feeling of determination rose within me. "We're going to drop our load right down those smokestacks," I thought to myself. Certainly, as I looked at those three young men that night, each one filled with adrenalin and dreams, I would have never believed it had I been told that two of them would die the next day.

After a good night's sleep in the makeshift tent barracks at the base, I got up in the early hours of August 20, 1944, to a clear bright dawn. The quiet hush that always seems to accompany early morning activities was broken by occasional banter and laughter as more than a hundred men made their preparations for the mission. By the time we were served our breakfast of eggs and Chinese-style black coffee, the mood in the mess hall had become subdued. We went through motions we'd gone through hundreds of times before. Nothing was different, yet everything was different.

When it was time to man the planes, the ground crew latched Sam Nixon into his cramped tail gunner's position at the rear of the plane. We expected to be in the air at least seventeen hours before Sam would get a chance to stretch again. The rest of us settled into our usual routine preflight checklists, except for Bud Roberts, who had to stop first to pick up his bombsight.

The mood in the plane was sober, as if a chill had descended over us. As usual, there was little chatter, each man quietly attending to the tasks at his station. Flying a B-29 was always serious business, but today, the mood was even more quietly intense than usual.

A view of the greenhouse of a B-29 during a bomb run. The bombardier in the nose is looking through a Norden bombsight. The co-pilot is shown on the right.

As planes began to roll, Rewitz and I kept an eye on the progress of the planes moving down the ramp. We had to be ready when our turn came. We were within sixty miles of the Japanese lines, and there was to be absolutely no radio communication, even at the field. Every move we made would be made by the clock, according to a minutely defined schedule. There would be no order to "Roll" coming from the tower.

Our orders were to fly most of the day in groups of four in loose formation, pulling in and tightening the formation at a specified location en route as we approached the target. We were assigned the number four position in a group led by our new squadron commander, Lt. Colonel Savoie.

The number one plane always flies the point position. If you think of a formation as a diamond, number one is in front, number two is to the right and slightly back, number three is to the left of the point, but slightly behind number two, and number four brings up the rear, slightly below the others. To get into formation, we took off at one-minute intervals. As soon as the first plane became airborne, it flew straight and level for four minutes, marked from the end of the runway, and then turned back toward the field. The second plane flew straight and level for three minutes before turning, and the third plane flew two. As the fourth plane started to turn at one minute, all four planes were at the same spot and ready to fall into formation and head toward the target.

The first planes out had stirred up the usual troublesome dust, and by the time our group began to taxi into position, the dust was boiling off the strip and visibility was poor. A slight crosswind helped a little. Dust blanketed the planes, and they loomed through the swirling yellow soup as brown silhouettes. Even with the roar of hundreds of powerful engines being started and revved, and the throbbing of the planes leaving the field, the noise was somehow muffled by pre-mission anxiety. We must succeed.

We took off without incident and settled into formation according to plan, beginning a long, slow climb to elevation. This time our slow climb to elevation wasn't due to being overloaded, it was because we were trying to conserve fuel. Our target was eight-and-a-half hours away, which meant an eight-and-a-half hour return. There wasn't a lot of slack for unforeseen fuel-consuming events such as a strong headwind or going off course to avoid fighter confrontation. Every aspect of the mission bespoke the fact that we were stretching to the outside limits of our range.

It took us seven hours to reach the China Sea, practically all of it over Japanese-occupied territory. The weather was clear, and we could look down and see the Japanese fighter fields below us. It was almost like watching a movie of little toy planes as they scrambled to get airborne and intercept us. Though we were still climbing, we knew we were too high and too fast for them to catch us. The real Japanese fighter threat would be over Japan, itself, where they flew high-performance Zeros. The fighters deployed on the fields below were older, fixed gear models, and not nearly as fast as a Zero.

Midway across the China Sea, we approached a large Japanese convoy. They started shooting their big guns at us, so our leader pulled off course a bit, skirted the convoy, then resumed course. Over the intercom we speculated that they were probably heading toward Manchuria.

While still over the sea, about thirty minutes away from the coast of Japan, our number two plane peeled off and headed back to base. With the radio silence, there was no way of knowing why, nor did it matter. We just pulled up from number four and flew the number two position in what was now a three-plane formation.

By now we were moving into a tighter, protective formation. Our wing tips were within fifty feet of each other. The coast of the Japanese island of Kyushu marked our I.P., or Initial Point, and we began our turn toward the target. Our orders were to check our guns at the I.P. or shortly thereafter. In a fluke of fate, some shell casings from the number one plane shattered our Plexiglas and we lost pressure. We immediately put on our oxygen masks. We had about a half hour to go before we reached the target.

A few minutes later, someone came over the intercom. "Lookie there. Parachutes. I pity those poor devils." Far below, were small white circles of silk. Our squadron wasn't in the first element. Whoever was down there had been shot down minutes before we arrived. They were some of those "others" to whom such unfortunate things happened.

National Archives

The Imperial Iron and Steel Works in Yawata, Japan. Taken during the attack on Yawata, August 20, 1944.

We began our approach into the target. Kennard punched speed, wind direction, and temperature data into the onboard computer as Roberts prepared the Norden bombsight. On this mission we were not to use the autopilot to control the aircraft during the bomb run. Instead, the lead plane established the direction to the target, and the rest of the planes in the formation followed. By having the pilots manually fly through the bomb runs, keeping the speed and direction constant, the bombardiers could concentrate on distance and, we hoped, obtain more precise releases.

We were over the target, straight and level. I could see smoke rising toward us in a black billowing cloud. There were bombs hitting those structures.

Suddenly I heard our right gunner, Bishop, and Armstrong, our senior gunner, talking excitedly over the intercom. They were both shooting at fighters. "A thousand yards out," I heard one of them shout. I could hear the guns firing.

One of the Zeros, though, wasn't shooting back. He stayed right off our wing tip, just out of range of the guns, relaying our altitude and speed to the antiaircraft installation below. Ahead of us, I could see the ominous black clouds that indicated flak bursts. The Zero peeled away.

We were flying straight and level. The target was below. "Bombs away," Roberts' voice crackled in my ear. I could feel the plane as it lifted in response to the release of our six five-hundred-pound bombs. One minute to go, straight and level.

Straight and level. By now the antiaircraft guns on the ground had determined our altitude and were sending up walls of exploding flak. I could feel the plane being jolted and shaken by the percussion of the explosions around us.

Would this last minute of the bomb run never end?

I asked Nixon in the tail if he could see where the bombs were hitting. He took a long time answering and mumbled something I couldn't make out.

We maintained our tight formation. I was sitting probably a hundred feet from the copilot of the number one plane. His name was Tom Young. Suddenly, something hit us. I must have momentarily lost consciousness from the impact, although in my memory, the events unfolded in a fast continuous stream. For Young, a stone's throw away, had thought he'd seen me die that day. Fifty years later, he told me with tears in his eyes, having just found out that I had not died in those moments, that he was looking out the window at our plane when it was hit just under the nose and right wing. There was a sudden, bright flash that filled the greenhouse and he saw me hurled against the Plexiglas, my face mashed against it. The last he saw of me, I was slumped in my seat, head hanging toward my lap.

I recall no flash. Just a loud noise and the forward pressure cabin filled with smoke. The heat was unbearable, intense, and it was all around us. I know now, that had we not lost oxygen earlier, forcing us to put on the oxygen masks that protected our lungs from the blast, those of us in the forward cabin probably would have been killed immediately.

Everyone was moving and shouting, and in the confusion, everything happened so fast. I could see Roberts, obviously in pain, trying to crawl over the top of the control panel. He was dragging his foot, which had been nearly blown off. I knew that something was wrong with me, too. I was aware of incredible pain. My right hand and arm were especially bad, but I didn't know why. I kept thinking, "Can we fly this out of here? We've got to fly this out of here."

But the plane was on fire. We couldn't survive in the cockpit, and so another voice rang out in my head that said, "We've got to bail out or we'll die." The battle to save the plane and get the crew back safely to China raged in my head with the voice that said, "Bail out." But my body sprang into action without listening to any voice. I hit the alarm bell. Bud Roberts had already crawled to the nosewheel door, our escape hatch, and had lifted the cover. I heard myself get on the intercom and give the order to evacuate. "Bail out. Quick. Everyone get out as best as you can." I waited long enough to hear acknowledgments from the rear, and at the same time pushed the switch to lower the nose gear so those of us in the forward cabin could get out through the hatch. The men around me were choking and gasping in the smoke and intense heat. We had to get out fast, but instead of the whine of the nose gear dropping out of the well, we only heard a tremendous clanking and grinding noise coming from the bottom of the plane. Clearly the motor and all controls had been damaged in the blast.

The men crowded forward as Kennard and I leapt into the wheel well, frantically trying to push the jammed gear down by jumping up and down on it, or standing on it trying to push against the wheel well to make it go down. When we could see a narrow opening to squeeze through, Kennard and I grabbed Roberts, his foot gushing blood, and pushed him out, motioning for the rest of the men to follow. Time was running out. Kennard and I squeezed through the opening and jumped out as quickly as we could to get out of the way, as Rewitz and Kazarian were already crawling down into the well. I expected that Robins was right behind them.

As my body dropped from the plane, I felt enormous relief. I had been afraid that we wouldn't be able to get the nose gear down and felt fortunate that Kennard and I had managed to budge it at all. The men in the rear pressure cabin had acknowledged the command to bail out, so I had reason to hope that the entire crew had managed to get out of the plane.

Everything we had been told about bailing out over Japan clicked into my mind. Because we were jumping from high altitude, twenty-six thousand feet, we knew to freefall for as long as possible. The goal was to get below the fighter plane level so the fighters wouldn't swoop by and pick us off in the chutes. I couldn't see any of the other men. They could be anywhere, above or below me, and I fell and fell and fell.

The wind against my body was so strong, the skin pulled tight against my skull, squeezing my eyes into watering slits. I kept trying to close my mouth, but my jaw was pulled open with such force, that no matter how I tried, I couldn't force my teeth together.

I could feel my clothes pulling against my body. It was almost as if someone had attached pins to the fabric and I was hanging, suspended in my clothing. I was certain that my clothes would shred and blow off me, they pulled so tight against the front of my body.

Our flight suits came equipped with a bail-out bottle, which would have provided me with oxygen if I had just managed to reach the tube and put it in my mouth. I didn't even try. Too much going on, and how would I close my mouth around it, anyway?

I kept falling.

Finally, it looked like time to pull the rip cord. I estimated that I had already fallen ten thousand feet. I struggled to bring my arm forward to reach the cord, and as soon as I pulled, I could hear the chute riffle out above me and snap full. I was falling at more than 120mph at this point. The harness jerked me severely as the parachute canopy snapped open, shooting blinding pain through my chest and legs.

As I recovered and began to drift in the wind, I was able to look at the city spread out below me. Yawata was located on a large bay. There must have been twenty or thirty big warships in the harbor. Our target, the enormous Imperial Iron and Steel Works, was at one end of the bay. I could see the large concrete buildings of the commercial areas, and the tightly packed single-story buildings that marked the residential zones.

We had been over water when we bailed out, but it was clear that I was now drifting toward a residential area. I thought about all the propaganda I'd seen and heard regarding the Japanese. I had every reason to believe that I was falling into a city of heartless, inhuman barbarians. I was terrified.

At some point after my chute opened, I realized that I was still wearing my flak helmet. It had flaps that came down over my earphones, and suddenly I wanted to be rid of it. I started to throw it down, and then paused, thinking, "Falling from this height, this thing could really hurt someone on the ground if it hit them."

Then, the lack of logic struck me. These were the people we were bombing. These were the enemy. I hurled the helmet toward Earth.

As I started to fall more slowly, the pain throughout my body hammered into my consciousness. I looked at my hands, searing in pain, and could see that the flesh had been burned off. From the feel of my arms and legs, I knew they were severely burned, too. Later, I would realize that I also had a flak fragment, the size of a nickel, imbedded in my thigh. It would be hours, though, before I would be able to focus on these injuries.

Below my feet was an alarmingly foreign-looking land. I was falling into a congested residential area. More than a hundred angry-looking, shouting people were out in the street watching as I fell toward them. Except for a few soldiers in uniform, they all appeared to be civilians and were waving wooden sticks and clubs of all shapes and sizes.

As I drew nearer, they formed a ring in the middle of the street. I could see that I was going to fall right into the middle of it.

Capture

"Behind the crashing airplane, we saw opening parachutes and evil Americans who wanted to save their lives."
Eyewitness account of August 20 B-29 raid over Yawata, Japan.
Mainichi Shimbun, Tokyo newspaper, August 21, 1944

As the ground and the circle of angry faces rushed up toward me, all I could think was, "Oh, damn."

I knew I could expect hostility and beatings on the ground, that was bad enough, but from the looks of the mob, it was clear that my death was just minutes away. I was powerless. I couldn't evade them and I couldn't protect myself.

In the final seconds before I hit the ground, I tried to position my feet beneath me, flexing my knees to absorb the impact. It was a futile attempt. I crashed into the pavement and tumbled, uncontrollably, for several feet. My survival pack burst open and scattered its contents in a trail behind me. When I stopped, I caught sight of my service 45mm pistol, within reach. While I was tempted, I didn't try to grab it. The mob was closing in, but I could see soldiers using the butts of their rifles to clear the crowd out of the way so they could get to me. I slowly stood up and raised my hands in surrender. I was unspeakably afraid and knew I was going to die right then.

Almost immediately, something hit me in the back of the head. Hard. It was probably the butt of a military rifle. It knocked me to the ground and I passed out.

As I regained consciousness, I was aware that I was being beaten where I lay. The mob had pressed in close. While it was clear that the soldiers were trying to push the crowd back, blows crashed down on me from all sides. My back, legs, arms, head, everything was under attack at once. I could hear each blow resonate through my body as the layers of pain increased. Everyone, male and female alike, was screaming and pushing at one another, each one eager to have a hand in my murder. I tried to draw myself into a ball and cover my head.

Somehow, a couple of soldiers got me to my feet and started to drag me through the crowd while others beat the screaming civilians back. Even though I was groggy, I could see that the blows the soldiers were landing with their rifle butts were brutal. What kind of a place was this? People were screaming and pointing at me, still struggling to land blows. The soldiers shouted and punched them back with their rifle butts. I was surrounded by voices, but could understand none of them. The soldiers finally won out and we were able to proceed up the street on foot, leaving the growling mob behind.

By this time, it was getting dark. The guards tied my hands behind my back. My burns hurt as if I was still on fire, and my whole body ached, but I could walk without assistance. The small single-story houses crowded up to the streets. The contrast between our safe, familiar Reddy Teddy and this strange land with its unusual buildings and violent people no doubt added to the disorientation I felt as my head slowly cleared.

I wished I were anywhere else. What in the world was I doing in this mess?

We went a few more blocks through the narrow streets, climbing a small hill, and stopped in front of a large, two or three-story wooden building. The thought flashed through my mind that the rest of the crew might be here. My jellied brain was starting to solidify again as the guards propelled me toward the door. "This must be some kind of headquarters," I thought.

Just outside the door, a small man in uniform stopped us. By his uniform, I gathered that he was a high-ranking naval officer. He stood in front of me, looking up. His face could hardly contain his hate for me.

"Do you see green in my eyes?" he asked in English.

"No," I answered. His fist crashed into my jaw before I could even flinch.

"Now do you see green in my eyes?" he asked again.

"Yes, sir."

The second blow was even harder than the first. I guess his need to participate in my punishment was satisfied. He stepped aside and my guards and I entered the building.

The place was in absolute pandemonium. It was teeming with uniformed personnel who could have been police, military, or members of the Kempe Tai. They all seemed highly agitated and confused, and there was much shouting and milling about.

The guards had me take off my flight suit and then relieved me of my uniform belt and anything remaining in my pockets. They tied my hands behind my back again and then took me upstairs into a large room where several Japanese officers and guards awaited me. I caught a glimpse of some parachutes and gear from other crew members strewn on the floor in one corner. The walls were lined with pictures of what must have been important Japanese military officers.

By this time, I was feeling more alert. It was clear that they were going to interrogate me. Each guard held a heavy wooden flattened club shaped like a Samurai sword. Each "sword" was several feet long and at least an inch thick. I couldn't imagine what these fake swords were for. Five or six officers sat facing me from behind a long row of tables. It was obvious by their uniforms and demeanor that they were high-ranking, but even they were clearly agitated and seething with hate.

My guards brought me to stand in front of one of the officers. He spoke excellent English, and had a long list of questions for me. These were definitely professionals. They'd done this kind of thing before and they knew just what they wanted to learn that night.

"Where did you take off from?" the interrogator asked. I had been briefed that when interrogated, we were to answer with only our name, rank, and serial number.

"First Lieutenant Ernest A. Pickett, serial number 0677559," I answered.

Crash! Something hit me from behind. I fell to the floor, dazed. The guards grabbed me and jerked me back to my feet.

"Where is your base?" the interrogator asked.

"First Lieutenant Ernest A. Pickett, serial number 0677559."

Crash! Again, the blow from behind. Only this time, it was followed by additional blows after I'd fallen. The guards were beating me with their heavy wooden swords. These were much more effective than anything I'd been hit with in the street.

The officers all started talking at once, gesturing and yelling. As I was pulled to my feet, the English-speaking officer stood and screamed at me.

"You will answer! Japanese government does not adhere to the terms of the Geneva Convention and will not accept these responses. Where is your base?"

"Mongolia," I lied.

The officers began speaking at once. Each one had questions they wanted to ask me. They addressed me in Japanese and the English-speaking officer translated. I knew that they couldn't yet have much information about the B-29 and I was determined not to tell them anything that would put any of the boys back at the base in additional peril. They wanted to know how large the base was, what our mission orders were, where I had trained in the United States, and my best friends' names. They had many questions about the B-29. It didn't seem to matter how I answered. To them, every question posed was an excuse for the guards to pummel me with the wooden swords. The blows went deep. I was amazed that my bones weren't breaking. Pain swept through my body in continuous waves.

After a few questions, which I tried to evade or answered with lies, they began alternating beatings with new techniques to get me to talk. They brought out two sets of wooden clamps, one for each hand. Each clamp was made of five long pieces of wood which they threaded vertically between my fingers. Two long bolts connected the pieces of wood along the tops and undersides of my fingers. At the end of each bolt was a large thumb screw for tightening the clamps. I could hardly open my right hand as swollen as it was from the burns, but they managed to jab the clamp into place anyway. At each question, they turned the screws on the clamps. The pressure on my knuckles was so intense, I knew something had to give soon. My skin turned clammy and cold as a knuckle broke, and then another.

I grew weaker as the interrogation and beatings continued into the night. I had begun by standing, but after a while, I just stopped getting up and sat or knelt on the floor as the questions kept coming. I interpreted each question as a direct threat to the safety of my friends and all the Americans involved in the B-29 effort.

As my hate for my interrogators and my fear of them grew, so did my determination to protect my comrades. Still, I knew that unless I wanted to die right there, I was going to have to keep coming up with some kind of answers to the questions. Each reply was a careful dance between my sense of loyalty and duty and my need for self-preservation.

I desperately wanted to live, yet I also knew that I couldn't save myself by telling them what they wanted to know. At some point in the interrogation, the English-speaking officer had screamed at me in frustration, "All B-29 people are criminals and will be executed." While the interrogators were highly emotional, I knew deep down that he believed he was speaking the truth. I had no reason to believe he was in error. If I was going to die anyway, I could see no point in exposing our men to danger by telling the enemy any secrets.

I don't know how many times I was beaten unconscious that night. I know I was in and out several times. Still, somehow, when I was awake, I felt clear-headed. I'd come to, there'd be another question, I'd evade it or lie or say as little as possible, then I'd find out how well I had managed to prolong my life for a few minutes by the severity of the next beating or torture.

While I prayed for the beatings to end, the alternatives were equally brutal. One of the guards tried using his cigarette to induce me to give a little more information. He stood at my back and with an astounding thoroughness, question by question, pressed the lit end of the cigarette into the back of my shirt until it burned through the cloth and made a series of smoldering craters across my shoulders and over my back. Through the pain, I could smell my flesh burning.

These people were animals, I concluded, and I despised them. In my eyes they were less than human. The propaganda had been accurate to depict them with bloody fangs and glaring insanity. I could see no sign of human goodness in these bloodthirsty savages.

I would not give them what they wanted. I hoped we bombed them into oblivion.

At some point during the interrogation, a photographer came in. My guards led me over to the corner in the back of the room where the gear was lying. They stood me in front of a window and had me turn to face the photographer. The guard on my left seemed to enjoy clamping down on my burned left hand. There was no skin left on it, and he repeatedly grabbed the rawest part. Two or three other guards stood behind us holding up a parachute, presumably mine. I'm certain the flash went off, but I don't recall many more of the details. My mind was filled with what lay on the plank floor a few feet in front of me.

The floor was covered in blood. Bud Roberts, our bombardier, my pinochle buddy, the guy who loved everyone, was lying on the floor, dead. His body was pointed away from me, and I couldn't see much of his head, but I could see more of his legs than I might have wanted. His injured foot had been cut off above the ankle. There was no tourniquet or bandaging on the wound, and it was

Ernest Pickett and four of his guards on the night of his capture in Yawata, Japan. Two of the guards are holding a parachute behind him. As the photo is taken, Pickett is looking at Roberts' body which is lying on the floor just a few feet away. The photograph ran in the Mainichi Shinbun *newspaper the following day.*

clear he had been left to bleed to death. His flak helmet, with his name stenciled onto the front of it, lay on the floor at my feet.

In my exhaustion and pain, I was still overwhelmed by fear and filled with hate, but as I looked at Bud's body, another emotion rose in me: despair. "Bud's already dead," I said to myself. "That's one down."

The interrogation resumed. Bud's body remained behind me on the floor in the corner.

As the hours blurred onward, I abandoned my attempts to sit up after the beatings. I lay on the floor, looking up at the bare-bulbed electric lights, fighting to stay alert to keep the dance of wits going.

They brought out blueprints of the B-29 for me to look at. I might as well answer their questions, they told me. They were going to find out what they wanted to know, anyway. "Yes, that is a B-29," I agreed, reeling that someone had betrayed us by providing the enemy with blueprints. Could I explain a certain feature, they asked. My vague answers didn't satisfy.

I was made to kneel in front of the interrogation table, hands again tied behind my back. With no skin on my hands, even the rope scraping across the raw tissue was a torture. They brought out a long heavy bamboo pole and placed it directly behind my knees as I knelt. To my horror, two guards came forward and stood on the pole, one on each end. I was blinded with pain. As I refused to answer each question, the guards standing on the pole beat me with their wooden swords until I passed out, which, mercifully, didn't take long. But each time I awoke, the pole was replaced and the beatings continued.

I wished I would hurry up and die.

"Where is your base?"

"Mongolia."

Maybe this time they'd hit me hard enough and it would be over.

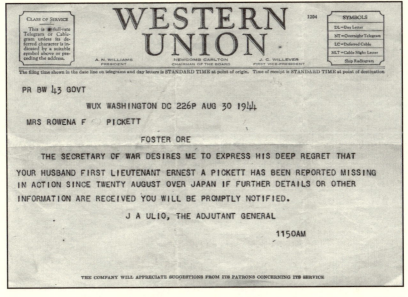

WESTERN UNION

CLASS OF SERVICE

This is a full-rate Telegram or Cablegram unless its deferred character is indicated by a suitable symbol above or preceding the address.

1204

A. N. WILLIAMS PRESIDENT
NEWCOMB CARLTON CHAIRMAN OF THE BOARD
J. C. WILLEVER FIRST VICE-PRESIDENT

SYMBOLS

DL=Day Letter
NT=Overnight Telegram
LC=Deferred Cable
NLT=Cable Night Letter
Ship Radiogram

The filing time shown in the date line on telegrams and day letters is STANDARD TIME at point of origin. Time of receipt is STANDARD TIME at point of destination

PR BW 43 GOVT

WUX WASHINGTON DC 226P AUG 30 1944

MRS ROWENA F PICKETT

FOSTER ORE

THE SECRETARY OF WAR DESIRES ME TO EXPRESS HIS DEEP REGRET THAT
YOUR HUSBAND FIRST LIEUTENANT ERNEST A PICKETT HAS BEEN REPORTED MISSING
IN ACTION SINCE TWENTY AUGUST OVER JAPAN IF FURTHER DETAILS OR OTHER
INFORMATION ARE RECEIVED YOU WILL BE PROMPTLY NOTIFIED.

J A ULIO, THE ADJUTANT GENERAL

1150AM

THE COMPANY WILL APPRECIATE SUGGESTIONS FROM ITS PATRONS CONCERNING ITS SERVICE

Telegram received by Faye Pickett telling of her husband's capture. While there was never official word from the Japanese that Ernest A. Pickett was a prisoner of war, the International Red Cross reported that a pilot, an Ernest Bicket, had been mentioned in the Japanese media as being captured during the Yawata raid. This small piece of information provided hope to those at home that Ernest was alive.

The Kempe Tai

"Terror upon terror overwhelms me, it sweeps away my resolution like the wind, and misery has me daily in its grip."

Job 30:15

When the long night of questions finally ended, I was taken into an empty room where I collapsed onto the bare wooden floor. It had probably been twenty hours since we left China, but it felt like days. The adrenaline that had kept me surprisingly alert for my interrogations was gone. I'd had no food or water since my arrival in Japan, but I didn't have energy to even wish for some. In my exhaustion and pain, I fell asleep immediately. If I was going to die that night, they could just kill me while I slept.

The next two or three days were a hellish blur. Except when taken out for additional interrogations, which lasted for hours at a time, I stayed alone on the floor of that room. There was no pillow or blanket, no furniture. I don't remember eating or going to the bathroom, although I must have done these things.

I had no will to get up and walk around. I hurt everywhere, constantly. Every slight movement sent spikes of pain through a hundred pulverized locations. My joints were swollen and stiff, my head hurt, and I was aware of an oozing gash on my face, but the burns from the explosion in the plane were the worst. Somehow, the blast had burned me right through my clothing. My shirt and pants were mostly intact, but the skin underneath was destroyed. My arms were especially bad. The transparent dead skin hung down in long shredded strips well past the tips of my fingers. My right hand was a raw shiny grey color, rigid and unresponsive on the end of my arm.

I needed medical attention, but none was forthcoming. Nor was I given clean clothing or allowed to wash myself. Instead, I only got the endless interrogations and continued beatings. I didn't know if I was going to live or die from hour to hour. I wondered if the Japanese didn't decide to kill me outright, how long it would take me to die of my injuries. As much as possible, I slept. My body demanded it, and I welcomed it as both a dulling of the gripping pain and as a temporary freedom from fear. But in my grudging periods of groggy wakefulness, I knew that survival wasn't possible.

One evening, two guards came into my cell and, by gestures, ordered me to my feet. I struggled to get up as quickly as possible to avoid a beating. Again, my crippled hands were tied behind my back. One of the guards was carrying what looked like a soft-sided woven basket. This he put upside down over my head. It made an effective blindfold. A little light came in from the bottom and I could see the front of my uniform and a few inches of floor, but I couldn't see anything through the tight weave of the basket. By tilting my head back or to the side I could catch small glimpses of my surroundings.

This must be it. They were going to kill me. I had no reason to think that the Japanese had anything better in store for me, and panic rose in my throat. I stood quietly, though. "These animals might kill me," I thought, "but I refuse to give them what they want."

The guards led me out of the building and stuffed me into the back seat of some kind of vehicle. I assumed it to be a staff car or something similar. A guard got in on either side of me and the car started forward. My brain battled against being overwhelmed by the unrelenting agony pounding through my body, yet, as it had in my interrogations, some part of my mind snapped into focus. I was aware and alert. I was struck by the sense of being in a metropolis. The car alternately slowed and surged forward through congested streets. I could hear other traffic and city noises around me. We could only have driven a mile or two before we pulled to a stop and the engine was turned off.

The guards pulled and jabbed me out of the back seat and I came to an unsteady stand next to the car. We immediately set off down some kind of sidewalk with each guard firmly gripping one arm. It was difficult walking with the woven hood. It was already dark out and while I could see a little through the bottom of the basket, I couldn't see enough to keep from tripping. The guards' rough grip, though, propelled me forward at a pretty good clip. I somehow managed to keep my feet under me.

From sounds and smells, I knew that we were near the bay. We only walked a short distance before we boarded some kind of water craft and sat down, my guards still on either side of me. We were on the deck of a heavy boat, and by the sound of the engine as it started up and the motion of the boat, I guessed that we were on a small harbor tug or something similar.

Two or three crewmen called out to one another. I could hear the crew moving about the boat, but there didn't seem to be any other passengers on board. If there were, they were staying quiet and still. As we set out across the bay, vibrations rumbled through me as the big engine churned through the water.

After about an hour, we pulled into a dock and once again I was escorted into the back seat of a car. Again we wormed our way through traffic and stopped after a few miles. When we got out this time, I was aware of a lot of activity around me. We were in a crowd of people. I could hear Japanese voices, male and female, moving in all directions.

The echoing voices told me we were in a large high-ceilinged building. It turned out to be a train station. My guards spoke no English, but by pushing and pulling on me, they were able to get me onto a train with little trouble. We made our way to the back of the car and the three of us sat down, with me in the middle.

At first, my hood stayed on. I could tell by the puff-puff of the engine and a glimpse of steam filtering back to us that we were being pulled by a steam engine. We were obviously on a civilian train that made a lot of stops. I could feel the train slow and stop and then passengers around us would get off while others got on. As the night wore on, I sometimes nodded off, letting my head drop forward onto my chest. I assume that my guards took turns doing the same.

If I gestured to the guards that I needed to go to the bathroom, they both took me down the aisle to the train lavatory. After untying my hands, one of them stayed with me even while I relieved myself.

My guards and I sat in those same seats at least two nights and most of three days. Eventually, they took my hood off and left my hands untied. The guards spoke to one another, and sometimes other military personnel might stop and talk with them for awhile. Aside from trying to tell me to do something, the guards made no attempt to communicate with me. None of the other passengers bothered us. I must have been a hideous sight, unshaven and dirty with my blood-stained clothing and seeping burns, but none of the civilians dared to look at me for long or ask questions of my guards. Watching them, I could see that the civilians were fearful of the military. It was such a contrast to the relationship between civilians and soldiers back home.

The guards took turns fetching food for us at meal times. One of the guards would make his way down the aisle and later return with three little wooden boxes and three pairs of chopsticks.

The little boxes were perhaps seven by five inches, and two inches deep, with a sliding wooden top. Inside were strips of daikon radish on top of a little bit of awful rice. Terrible tasting. Fortunately, I didn't have much appetite. The stress of my situation and the strangeness of the food left me with little desire to eat. I would have had trouble choking the stuff down under the best circumstances, but my crippled right hand made matters much worse. The guards showed me how to hold the chopsticks, but my hand was burned so deeply that I could only make a kind of claw out of it. It shook violently if I tried to use it at all, so I tried the chopsticks in my left hand. It wasn't very effective. Eating with my fingers wasn't even an option. My hands were filthy. I hadn't been allowed to wash them since my capture.

By the last day on the train, I could tell that we must be nearing a large city. There were lots of stops and more people got on and off. The train became increasingly crowded. At last we pulled to a stop and after having my hands retied and the hood replaced, we got off the train. By the sounds and crush of people, I guessed that we were in a major railway station. My guards maneuvered me through the crowd and into a waiting car which drove through what was obviously a large, bustling city.

Finally, the car pulled to a stop and I was taken, still hooded, into a building and turned over to new guards who bullied me roughly down a flight of stairs. From the dank chill air, I could tell I was in a basement. Very little light bled in from under the edge of my hood. I could tell there were other people in the area, but there was no talking, just an occasional sniffle or moan.

The new guards pulled off my hood in front of a small wooden door. They opened it to expose a dingy wooden box about eight feet square. The front and back was barred with four-by-fours spaced vertically a couple inches apart. The side walls were made of a thin lightweight lumber. A dim electric light hung from the center of the ceiling. The wooden floor of the cell was built up off the concrete and I had to step up and duck at the same time to squeeze through the small door as the guards pushed from behind.

From listening to the movement of the guards, I figured out that the row of cells was a long narrow island of sorts. The cells were built to adjoin one another, but the fronts and backs were open to a passageway that the guards strode up and down. I learned quickly that it was important to stay toward the middle of the box. The guards made it a habit to jab their bayonets or swords in through the wooden bars as they walked past. I felt like a caged animal.

The basement smelled like a sewer. I soon discovered why. There was a hole cut into the wooden floor of my cell. I assumed that all the cells were built the same way. Below the hole, placed between the cement floor and the elevated wooden floor was a foul wooden box. This was my toilet, the *benjo*. There was no toilet paper, no bedding, nothing. I stood there with almost a week's growth of beard, severely injured, not having seen a hairbrush, a toothbrush, or a bar of soap since China, and realized that things had just gone from bad to worse.

As I lay slumped down against the side of my cage, my eye caught some pencil marks on the wood. There were several American names, including the name Doolittle. By the dates next to some of them, I could only assume that some of the men who were shot down during Doolittle's famous raid over Tokyo years before had been held in this same cell.

As the footsteps of the guards receded down the passageway, I noticed some movement near a knothole on the other side of my pen. Someone was trying to get my attention. I crawled over to it and looked through. It was Kennard! Kennard was alive and in the cell next to me. While part of me rejoiced, the grim despair I'd felt in Yawata was still with me. Kennard was alive today, but how much longer would it be until he was dead?

He motioned that we had to be very quiet. He held his right arm up to the knothole. He was shaking and upset. Even in the dim light, I could scarcely believe what I saw. Kennard's arm had been nearly sliced off just below the elbow. He told me that when he was captured after the bailout, a soldier had run up to him with a Samurai sword. "He took a swipe at my head," Kennard whispered. He had thrown his arm up at the last instant to fend off the blow. It saved his neck, but the sword had cut through one bone of his forearm and part of the second. It was probably a week since our capture and the wound looked bad. The flesh had spread a couple inches apart and bone was lying exposed. "I can't use my hand at all," he told me, almost hysterical. He held it up to the knothole. It was beginning to curl inward. He, too, had received no medical attention.

"What are we going to do?" he whispered desperately. We heard guards' footsteps approaching and we quickly turned our backs and moved away from the knothole. As soon as the guards left, I returned. He was wild-eyed, frantic, crying. I wondered if he had been like this the whole time or if seeing me had made him fall apart. I tried to calm him and tell him we were going to be ok, although I couldn't blame him for not believing me.

I hadn't been in my cell long before two guards returned to take me elsewhere. The hood was replaced, my hands were tied, and they propelled me back upstairs. In a replay of my days in Yawata, my hood came off and I again found myself facing a long row of tables behind which sat a number of officers and an English-speaking interpreter. I was placed in a chair facing the tables. The interpreter informed me that I was in the military police headquarters in Tokyo, headquarters of the Kempe Tai. I was to learn during my time in Japan that the Kempe Tai had a reputation for brutality, even among the Japanese. Civilians, policemen, and even other military personnel feared the Kempe Tai and carefully avoided contact or any chance of giving offense. The Kempe Tai were liberal in applying beatings to anyone they encountered. Their will was law.

My interrogation began much like the interrogations I had endured in Yawata. The officers were clearly high-ranking and professional. They had specific things they wanted to find out. They asked a question and I responded with name, rank, and serial number. I was beaten senseless.

The guards seemed to relish any opportunity to pound me into the ground. To me, they were a pack of cruel, barbaric, animals. Nearly every question, every answer, was accompanied by a blow of some kind. The guards seemed to wait eagerly for each opportunity to attack. By this time, my hate for them was a steady, unwavering flame that strengthened me. As in Yawata, I was determined to remain loyal to my buddies who were still free. I was bound by a profound sense of duty. These Japanese were obviously going to kill me, anyway. My talking would not save my skin.

I evaded, I lied, I answered in vague generalities. They answered with rifle butts to the head, kicks to my stomach and groin, and every other variety of beating one can imagine. They repeated the tortures I'd experienced before. I alternately passed out and revived.

I quickly learned the routine at Kempe Tai. Every new day of the three or four weeks I was there meant another interrogation. They grilled me on everything. They wanted information about how our forces were organized, what our mission orders had been, and as always, they wanted details about the B-29. How fast could it fly? How many bombs could it carry? What was its range? Where were the bases? How many planes were there? Every day meant a beating that left me barely able to crawl into my cell.

But while I strove to frustrate the attempts of my interrogators, I learned valuable information from them. At one point they were pressing me for some detail and they told me that, "Lieutenant Humphrey told us otherwise." Humphrey had been there! At least he had been captured alive and survived long enough to make it there. There was hope that he was still living. He might even be there now. If only we had had a chance to collaborate on our stories, we both might have been spared a couple of beatings.

Even with the prohibition against speaking, those of us in the basement cell block found small ways to communicate. Because each man was hooded and taken out for interrogation every day, there were two times a day when each person had a small opportunity to mumble something as he passed in front of the barred cages. While we couldn't see into the corridor clearly—the lights were dim in the dank basement and it certainly wasn't safe to go up to the front of the cages for a better look—we could catch glimpses. Maybe a man would mumble his name or make a comment to a Japanese-speaking guard that might reveal his hometown or the name of his airplane.

I came to believe that there were maybe forty or fifty men being held as I was, but I had no way of verifying that number or of knowing if there were prisoners in another area of the same building. I wondered about the other members of the crew and how they fared. Were they alive? I listened in vain to hear their names from the hooded figures that stumbled past my cell.

Still, these small moments of contact and introduction were priceless treasures. There was a bond between us. It made us feel less alone.

But in reality, each of us was painfully alone and vulnerable. Apart from the brief exchanges between Kennard and me through the knothole, there was no direct solace, no source of comfort. Even our cells were not safe havens, for the prowling guards made sport of unexpectedly throwing open the cell door, charging in and working the prisoner over unprovoked. It always happened so fast—the footsteps, the lurch of fear, and the vicious faces tower-ing from above just before the boot made contact with ribs.

One time my door flew open and instead of guards, a Japa-nese gentleman came stumbling in. He was a middle-aged man, clean and normal looking, wearing a civilian jacket and slacks. I couldn't imagine what he was doing there. He seemed as surprised to see me and quickly sat down against the wall as far away from me as possible. We made no attempt to communicate by gesture or language, but I soon figured out that he must be on trial for some-thing because he would be taken away for long periods of time and then returned. I noticed that he never appeared to be beaten up.

While I would later share my cell with other Japanese civil-ians for a few hours, this one stayed for a couple of days and made a profound impression on me. He seemed to be deeply ashamed for me to see him there. His body language, the way he avoided my gaze, and his agonized looks and sighs, belied a mood of complete disgrace.

By this time, I had been without sufficient food for long enough that I was constantly hungry. I hungrily gobbled up any-thing they gave me. Unfortunately, that usually meant a small bit of rice in a box that was shoved into my cell with a pair of chop-sticks a couple times a day. After the first day, the civilian must have been hungry, too. He had no more to eat than I did. Yet, twice, he took his box of rice, ate a couple of bites, and then, without making eye contact, handed his rice box to me.

I never knew his motive. I didn't know if he disliked the food or if his obvious humiliation at being in prison and the foul sur-roundings took away his appetite. But my feeling at the time was that he took pity on me and decided that as bad as his lot was, mine was worse.

It must have been awful for him to be locked up with me. I hadn't bathed in two or three weeks, was crawling with vermin, and smelled terrible. I couldn't hold the chopsticks and had to scoop the rice out of the little box with my dirty left hand. I was bearded and covered with oozing burns. The gash on my cheek had abscessed and had swollen up into a pus-filled lump the size of my fist. To talk or eat was painfully difficult and it must have also been awful to watch me. I interpreted his actions as kindness, but whatever his motivations, I was extremely happy to eat his rice.

Perhaps the abscess bothered my interrogators, too, for one day the door to my cell opened and to my shock, in came a Japanese doctor followed by a nurse holding a little cup. The doctor inspected the abscess and lanced it, after which the nurse held the cup to my face and let the abscess drain into it until the cup was full. Once the cup was filled, they both turned and left. It was very matter of fact and was over quickly. They applied no antibiotics or dressings to the wound.

This event amazed and confounded me because I knew of nobody else who had been visited by a doctor. As I had only seen savagery and sadistic brutality from my captors, this seemingly small, but inconsistent event left me bewildered. I had been in a lot of pain from the abscess, but I had many wounds that weren't receiving attention, so I expected no relief or treatment for my face. Still, it felt so much better.

To this day, I find this event puzzling. At the same time my face was swelling up, I was struggling with my burns which involved both hands, much of each arm and the length of both legs. The burns were repeating an endless cycle. A small crust would form over a raw area, temporarily sealing it. Then the swelling would start. The wound would swell and swell until the crust of new skin cracked. Pus dripped off the cracked areas continually, creating pools on the floor wherever I stopped. This included the floor of the interrogation room. The guards didn't hesitate to grab my sticky sleeves or my raw hands. The doctor and nurse didn't give a moment's attention to my burns.

They also didn't assist Kennard with his arm in any way. He was having a horrible time. I guessed that Kennard was going through alcohol withdrawal. Between the injury to his arm, the withdrawal, and the hellish nights and days we all endured, he was in bad shape. He spent endless hours in his cell, whimpering softly, obsessed with wanting sugar. He was desperate for sugar and he talked about it constantly, to himself, and to me whenever possible. He would call me over to the knothole. "Can you get me some sugar?" he'd plead, as though cajoling me or begging would make me suddenly able to fill his need. We couldn't speak freely to one another, but when there was an opportunity to whisper discreetly, I did what little I could to comfort him.

I had no idea how to help Kennard. I tried to encourage him to pull himself together as best he could. I truly believed that he would feel better if he could get himself under control a little more.

One day, I heard Kennard sobbing. I slipped over to the knothole and he held his arm up for me to see. His wound was full of maggots. Kennard was beside himself. I thought quickly and told him in as firm and calm a whisper as I could manage, "Leave them be. That's the best thing that could happen. They'll eat away the dead tissue and save your life."

It must have been horrible for him, but he left the maggots.

The daily interrogations and beatings continued.

"What were you bombing?" they asked.

"I was bombing the steel mill at Yawata."

"You dropped your bombs on the civilians."

"No. We were bombing the steel mill."

"What if the bombs hit among civilians? They couldn't come to work in the factories and the factories would have to shut down. Is that true?"

"That could happen." One day as I was escorted back to my cell, the guard told me my trial was over and that I had been found guilty.

"Trial?" I asked. I had not seen any evidence of a trial. I had certainly not had any legal representation or been allowed to offer testimony in my defense.

"You are tried as a criminal, not as a prisoner of war," he told me, "and now you will be executed."

Kinoshu

"…the bright day is done,
And we are for the dark."

William Shakespeare
Antony and Cleopatra

I had felt all along that I would die in Japan, but now I had no hope of surviving. Fear gripped me. I wanted to live. I wanted to go home. They were going to kill me and I couldn't have hated them more.

"Guilty of what?" I had asked the guard, but he hadn't said. Nor had he told me when I would be killed, only that I would be. Filled with horror, I entered my cell. From that moment, every time I heard footsteps approach, an intense spike of panic rose above the constant fear that left me trembling in my cell. Then, as the steps receded, I tried to calm myself. That wasn't it. It wasn't time, yet. Even the delivery of food or water caused a momentary panic to seize me.

Then one time, the footsteps stopped at my door and the door creaked open. Guards. They were there for me. I had heard other men taken out who seemingly had never returned. "Oh, my God. When am I going to wake up from this nightmare?" I thought to myself.

As I emerged from the box, the hood was placed over my head and we started down the corridor. Before long, I could tell that we were not taking the normal route to the interrogation room. So this was it. My mind was a jumble of thoughts, disbelief that this was happening, hate for the Japanese, regret at not getting to see Faye and my family and not getting to live the life I'd planned. And panic. But at some deep level, I also had that feeling of certain despair. I couldn't avoid this death. At least it would all be over. I was afraid of how I would die. I hoped it happened quickly and I prayed that they wouldn't torture me again.

Still hooded, I was escorted outside and put into a car with my guards alongside me. Where could we be going? The guards communicated nothing to me. Each moment was one of quaking torment.

Eventually the car stopped and I reluctantly got out. The guards yanked me along and up some steps into a building. After exchanging a few words with my guards, new guards took hold of me and led me away. This was where I was going to die, at any moment, and because of the hood, I couldn't even look around.

I was filled with despair. "Why?" was all I could ask myself. We had bombed targets in enemy cities just as the Japanese had done. "I was doing my job. They would have done the same," I said to myself. "How is it that I deserve to die?" I went as calmly as I could, grieving silently, "Why, why, why?"

To my surprise and relief, when they removed my hood, I was standing in front of a wooden cell door. A holding pen, I assumed. In the dim light, I could see a long row of pens, barred with wood at the front and back, much like those at Kempe Tai headquarters, but a little larger. We were on the ground floor of the building, but the only windows were small and placed high in the wall. It was dark and cold and smelly. The cells had the same lightweight ¼" lumber separating them that I had seen in use in so many buildings. It seemed such a strange building material. Wood must have been extremely scarce in Japan. The guard opened the door and motioned me inside.

The cell was six to eight feet wide, with a smelly *benjo* in one corner. The floor was covered with half-inch thick woven reed mats. I soon learned that these mats were alive with busy populations of lice and fleas. A dull electric bulb hung from the ceiling and would burn, I correctly guessed, continually, night and day. A standing water faucet stood to one side. Using my left hand, I turned the trickle of icy water on and ran my hands under it. I couldn't rub them because of the burns, but it felt good to at least rinse them. I splashed the cold water on my face. A small luxury.

As it turned out, three other men were also transported there that day. We all arrived separately, and as before, we couldn't see one another or communicate, but through our mumbles and move-ments, we knew of one another's presence.

The guards told us that we were being held at the Kinoshu Federal Penitentiary and that we were there awaiting execution. When we asked when the executions would occur, we were an-swered with a shrug and, "Any time."

By listening to the guards' footsteps as they paced the corri-dors that ran in front of and behind the cells, it was pretty clear that one or two empty cells—at least ten or fifteen feet—sepa-rated each of us four prisoners from the next man in the row. I was on one end of the group, to the right as we came in the door. There were several unoccupied cells beyond me, and I could hear the foot-steps of the guards as they turned the corner at the end cell and came back around the other side of the cell row. There was a man a few cells to the left of me and then another a few cells beyond him. The last man, fifteen or twenty cells away from me, was on the far end of the row and had a small window high up in the wall of his cell. There were other small windows along the wall in the corri-dors, which we could look up through and see the small squares of sky, but his was the only one attached to a cell.

We were the only prisoners in an area that would probably

have held one or two hundred easily.

Through motions and broken English, the guards soon let us know that we were not to move freely around the cells except to use the *benjo*. We were to sit on the filthy mats, backs against the grimy rough wooden wall, legs extending straight, arms resting straight ahead on our legs. Then, in prescribed intervals of probably thirty minutes, at a signal from the guard, we were to sit with arms and legs folded. Filled with the terrible anticipation of our pending execution, we alternated between these two positions as the fear-gripped minutes turned into hours.

The senseless shifts in posture continued and my muscles cried out to stretch and move around. With a sense of unreality, I found myself engaging in the mundane motions of existence: picking a flea off of me when the guards weren't looking, swatting a louse off my neck, going to the bathroom, gobbling down the small bit of rice they brought me, taking a drink from the faucet. It made no sense to do these things; they were coming to get me to kill me any minute. That was the big thing, yet my body carried on as if I might live into the next hour, as if there was a point to these activities and urges.

The hours ground on into night, and eventually the guards motioned for us to lie down. The quiet pacing of the guards continued around the island of cells and the bare bulb glared on through the hours, illuminating the hungry fleas and lice that were now teeming at eye level. The stillness was palpable. My ears were on alert, and even small, inconsequential shufflings and stirrings roared through my head. The stink of the *benjo* box and my own rancid skin and clothing consumed the breathable air. The guards paced their endless rounds and the night pressed down on my motionless body like a great weight.

Then, after an eternity, I sensed a small change. I looked at a window high in the wall across from my cell and watched as a small bleak square of morning came through it. There was no comfort in this dawn. My panic rose with the sun. I would die this day. They were going to kill me. I began to jump again at every sound. I tensed each time the guards approached my cell in their relentless orbits around the cell block. When I became too worn by panic, I fell into a withering, aching despair that consumed me.

They delivered another small box of rice, a *meshi* box. I was eating again. Why? Was this my last meal? The guards began the sitting regimen again.

The day lurched forward. "They'll do it first thing in the morning," I thought. Then as mid-morning passed, it seemed that immediately after lunch seemed likely. As mid-afternoon passed, I felt that surely they would come for us before the end of the day. It made no sense for them to prolong things. What were they waiting for? They had brought us to the penitentiary because this is where they executed people. I waited in agony, exhausting myself in an endless state of helpless agitation.

The day turned again to night. And that night was followed by another and another. There was no choice but to adapt to this new situation. They might kill me at any moment, but until that moment came, I had to continue living.

While the guards at Kinoshu were still clearly the enemy, they were not as hideous as the Kempe Tai personnel had been. The Kempe Tai looked for any opportunity to bully or hurt us. While these guards did their jobs, forcing us through the sitting routine during the day, and then making us lie down until the prescribed time of morning, overall they did not seem to have the same sadistic streak as their Kempe Tai brethren. They didn't beat us.

We fell into a habit of saying something to them when they walked past our cells. The man a few feet down from me was particularly chatty with the guards. He'd talk to them about anything, and they seemed to like the attention. Over time, some of them even became a little friendly, practicing their Pidgen English on us.

This willingness of the guards to engage us in conversation or to at least tolerate our comments enabled the four of us to keep in communication as the days slowly turned into weeks and then months. We always spoke up when we addressed the guards so our voices would carry to the end of the row. This wasn't too obvious, because the guards hardly spoke English and it's a normal impulse to raise your voice a little to communicate. Through this technique I learned the full names and ranks of the others. Second Lieutenant Irving Newman, the man in the cell closest to me, was a navigator from Boston and spoke with an East Coast accent. After him, down the row, was Colonel Richard Carmichael, a group commander. Throughout our ordeal, Carmichael kept a good attitude, which made things easier for all of us. At the end of the row in the cell with the window was Major Harold Mann, a group bombardier from Pennsylvania. He was pretty quiet and matter-of-fact.

We figured out between us that we were the highest-ranking surviving officers from four planes shot down on the August 20 Yawata raid. For this, we had received the death sentence. Knowing the identities and something about the other men eased the powerful sense of isolation I felt.

Talking through the guards didn't mean, though, that we could chatter away easily. They made it clear that we were not to talk to one another. The short bursts of disguised communication were the exceptions to our day, the bright spots, not the rule. We had no direct contact with our comrades. We never left our cells. Each of us was a faceless voice to the others, a disembodied presence that echoed weakly through the dark cell block. Our lives were suspended in time, ticking slowly away without purpose.

I found myself replaying the last minutes of the mission over and over in my mind. I blamed our commanders for what had happened to my crew and me. Had it not been for the long minute of straight and level flying after bombs away, we would have peeled off and been out of danger long before the flak could have hit us. It seemed such a terrible, pointless waste. I doubted that any of us would ever get home, and I grieved over the fate of my friends. And I grieved for me.

I began to use my thumbnail each day to make a scratch in the wooden floor, counting my days of imprisonment. Somehow, this act of forcing time into a familiar unit of measure let me feel some control and awareness over what would otherwise be only an endless succession of mind-deadening minutes. It might also have been a small statement of hope. Unless I eventually got out, it wouldn't matter how many days I was there.

The passing of time did nothing to ease my fear of execution. Any time an unrecognized set of footsteps approached, day or night, or there was a minuscule variation in the routine, I had to wrestle with panic. No amount of conditioning appeased this response. They were going to kill me, it was just a matter of when. They had said, "Any time." It made no time safe.

One day, Mann had a bit of news for us from his cell at the end of the row. The tiny window at the top of the wall of his cell had been open. Someone had pounded on the outside wall and thrown a rice ball inside. Mann was bewildered and grateful. Then a guard's voice had come through the open window and said in English, "Tomorrow you are executed."

Those moments of heightened terror poured through me like an icy sheet that seemed to drain all the blood out of my body in an instant. But none of us were killed the next day. Or the next.

Every tomorrow felt like a threat.

Still, we had a greater preoccupation than fear, isolation, and the physical breakdown caused by the sitting routine. We were starving to death. We were given a little bit of rice a couple of times a day which we ate, with chopsticks if able, out of the tiny *meshi* boxes. While we ate every grain of rice, it wasn't enough to fill us, nor did it contain enough nutritional value to sustain us despite our limited physical activity. It wasn't long before the effects of slow starvation began to tell on us all.

We lost fat first, of course, and our skin began to hang off our bones. Bowel movements were few and far between, and I could see my stomach becoming bloated. I tried to drink the cold water to satisfy the pain in my stomach, but it seemed to only sit in my gut and make it hurt more. I chewed each morsel of food slowly and thoroughly, not to savor it for the taste, but to help my body extract every possible bit of nutrition from it. There was a constant gripping ache in my bowels that made the endless minutes tick by even more slowly.

I often looked at the small square of sky that I could see through the high window outside my cell. I wondered what it would be like to breathe that clean air and to walk unhindered outside instead of being caged like an animal, starving, and filthy, alternating between a dull-eyed stare and fear. I thought bitterly that I wouldn't even reduce a dog to the state we were in, and my hatred of the Japanese knew no bounds.

I could see the seasons changing. The days grew shorter and the weather grew ever colder. The thumbnail scratches on my floor multiplied. I had been shot down in August. Fall was turning into winter. At least once, I saw snow fall. As the months marched on, the temperature plummeted in our cells. I was wearing only the filthy tattered uniform I had worn the day we were shot down. It had never been washed, or even removed. I would have loved to jump up and down or rub my limbs to get warm, but such movement would have only resulted in a beating. I was cold all the time. The continual violent shivering made my body ache. I grew steadily weaker as I began to lose muscle, my body converting every possible bit of flesh to calories.

As our captivity and isolation deepened, so did my retreat into myself. The starving mind does strange things to survive. For me, thoughts of home and family became dull and infrequent. At some level, I knew I wanted out, I knew I wanted to go home, but vivid or even cohesive thoughts about something so remote became nearly impossible. My mind seemed to be able to focus on only the most immediate issues of food, fear, and cold. Had it not been for that distant contact with the three men down the row, my mind might have retreated and shut down entirely in the endless monotonous march of minutes that made up hours, days, weeks, months.

Somehow, the four of us eventually developed a daily ritual together which became the focus of our hours. It allowed us to have bursts of being fully alive, once again human. We took turns "hosting dinner." At some point during the late afternoon, the "host" would engage a guard in conversation. Because the guards knew little English, it was a sort of game to throw out comments in such a way and with appropriate timing so we wouldn't get in trouble and could prolong the "meal."

"We'll start with warm creamy tomato bisque," the host might say as the guard passed by.

In the other cells, three minds immediately conjured up the sight, smell and texture of a warm rich soup.

As the guard sauntered over to check on the prisoner, the host might look at him and while showing him a scratch on his arm or pointing to the lice in the mats, he would go into great detail about the size of the chunks of tomatoes or the balance of spices that went into the mixture.

Soup was always served with crackers, but they were never just called crackers. They might be "saltines," for example, and every browned bump and grain of salt was described before we were allowed to feel the cracker melt away on our tongues as the guard took his slow turn around the cell block.

A little later, the guard might pass by the host cell and glance in, at which point the host would tell us about the salad we would have that night. We knew the color and size of every leaf, and the dressings were described in great detail. If we were lucky and had a chatty guard, we could get the description of all the radishes and cucumbers and other tidbits in the salad and could sit and savor our salads in splendor as the guard took his turn down the passage or visited with another guard.

It took us hours to "eat" every night, and our attention was riveted to our host the entire time. The dinners were magnificent. There were always hors d'oeuvres, and special beverages and desserts. Luscious steaks, potatoes and gravy, and pies hot out of the oven topped with ice cream filled our imaginations. All of the meals were described in elaborate and filling detail, some hearty and plain, some gourmet.

It became a game to outdo the previous meal, both in content and description. The host for the day could count on spending the hours before dinner in contemplation of what he would "feed" his guests that night. I have no doubt that this game helped us to maintain our sanity.

While our imaginary meals were helpful, we received a special meal from the Japanese one day. It was New Year's Day. "Everybody birthday in Japan today," our guard said. "*Omedetoo.*" We had a piece of pickled daikon that day and an extra share of rice which had little bits of fish mixed in. As hungry as I was, it would not have been hard to gobble the small meal down in a few bites, but I didn't. I chewed each bite slowly, savoring it for as long as I could, enjoying the sensation of feeding life into my body. But the wonder of all wonders was the tangerine. Despite my trembling, bent fingers, I peeled it painstakingly so that not a drop of juice escaped. And then I put a section into my mouth and bit down slowly. I couldn't believe how delicious it was. I chewed more slowly than I ever had, feeling each bit of juice as it went down my throat. After I'd chewed the piece carefully, I held it in my mouth for a long while. It was so good, I simply didn't want to swallow it.

The tangerine disappeared all too quickly. And then I ate the peel.

Survival became a daily conscious task. Small things, like the frequent minor earthquakes which rumbled through the building during our captivity, didn't even elicit comment. I had never been in an earthquake before, and one would think it would be a curiosity, but I never felt a big jolt or anything that would spur any kind of reaction on the part of the guards, and there were simply more important things to think about.

The physical challenge of living through each moment grew more taxing as the months passed. The temperature continued to plunge. I was growing gravely ill. My wounds had slowly begun to heal, layers of dead skin peeling away to reveal angry red scars along my limbs, but I had developed both wet and dry beriberi and had contracted dysentery. The beriberi caused severe painful swelling in my lower legs. Moving them to perform the sitting regimen was agony. The dysentery, though, with its associated cramps and diarrhea made getting up and down frequently a necessity.

"*Benjo kudasai?*" I requested of the guards repeatedly throughout the day.

"*Hai,*" they grunted in consent, and I'd slowly drag myself to my corner *benjo*. The dysentery was relentless and sapped any strength I might have been harboring. Because there was no toilet paper in my cell, the diarrhea only added to the caked-on filth that covered my infested body.

My mind turned inward to survive, to get through the day. I brought myself alert if I sensed danger, or to catch any bits of conversation from the men down the row. But soon, even this became too strenuous. I began to sit next to the foul *benjo* box, too weak to drag my body back and forth to relieve myself.

I had yet to see a blanket in Japan, but at some point, after I grew so sick and was so very cold all the time, I was given an old ragged faded brown garment. It looked like a heavy quilted bathrobe and I assumed it was a kimono. I was so happy to see it. I grabbed it immediately and put it on, shaking all the while. I felt warmer immediately. My violent shaking subsided and I could take a deep breath as its warmth encompassed me. The kimono was probably a half-inch thick. It had long sleeves and was about calf-length on me. I had to hold it closed as they gave me no belt or sash, but at that point I didn't care. It was saving my life. I wasn't warm yet, but it made a huge difference. Without the kimono, I'm certain I would have frozen to death on the floor of my cell. But I wasn't out of the woods yet.

As my starvation and illness grew more profound, my very existence became a dim, vague concept even to myself, as if my brain were saving energy by shutting down as much as possible. There were brief sparks of attention when I thought I might be in danger or when I thought there was a possibility of getting more food, but eventually, even those stimuli failed to rouse me. I began to ignore the guards' orders to change position or to sit up. I was too weak. I was dying.

My salvation came in the form of a Japanese doctor who came in to examine me. He spoke no English, but seemed quite stricken by my condition. As I lay inert before him, I could see the anger in his expression deepen the more he saw. I was too weak to try to communicate with him in any way or care if he was trying to communicate with me, but my sense of him was one of comfort and concern.

When he finished his brief examination, he called roughly to the guards to leave. I could hear his angry outburst as he left and moved down the corridor. I lay where he left me.

Later, two guards came and dragged me out of my cell and up the stairs. I was too weak to walk, too sick to even wonder where we were going. They didn't tie my hands and there was no hood this time. Before I knew it, we had burst into the fresh outside air. The light was blinding at first. The assault of new smells and sounds, after the months in my cage, both startled and revived me. I gulped huge lungfuls of the sweet air. I looked around me. We were in a small town, perhaps a suburb. There wasn't a civilian in sight. The guards continued their grip on my arms as I struggled, weak-kneed, down the sidewalk between them. We walked a block or two before entering a building.

I found myself standing in a spacious wood-lined room. In the middle of the open room was a large square wooden vat filled with steaming water. There was no one in the building but the guards and me. The air was muggy and warm. Arranged around the tub were stands for soap. I was in a community bath house.

Despite my weakness, I somehow managed to undress at the guards' prompting. They stood vigilantly near me, rifles and bayonets at the ready. Through their gestures, I understood that I was to take a bucket of steaming hot water from a nearby tub. I hadn't lifted anything in months, and it was a struggle to do as they ordered, but soon the bucket of water was standing at my feet. Using the water and a large bar of soap, I soaped my body, hair, and shaggily bearded face as long as my weakened state allowed.

I must have looked like Ben Gunn standing there, but I felt no self-consciousness or anxiety. I was getting clean. That was wonderful. If only I weren't so sick and could better enjoy it.

The guards then motioned that I was to rinse off using the water in the bucket. I somehow managed to hoist the bucket over my head and poured the hot water over me. Again, it would have been luxurious, except that the water was so hot. I flinched as it rushed over my skin.

Then the guards motioned me toward the big tub. I was to get in.

It was way too hot. I motioned that no, I couldn't get in. Too hot. They closed in with their bayonets, insistent. I had no choice. One way or the other, they were putting me in that tub. The water felt as if it must be reaching the boiling point. It seared my skin, especially when it hit the tender scar tissue that covered my burns. "All the way in," they motioned. I worried that I might pass out from the intensity of the pain as I submerged myself to the neck in that awful vat.

My impulse was to raise myself out of the water, to let my skin cool, but every time I made such a motion, the guards thrust the bayonets in my face and forced me back down. They had to see that I was in agony. I was clean, why did they have to torture me now?

They obviously had in mind a good long soak. It seems that my body should have adjusted to the water temperature after awhile, but the entire bath was an ordeal that seemed to last forever. I had been so cold for so long, and now getting warm was just as bad.

Eventually, they let me out. There were no towels. I climbed shakily back into my lice-infested clothing. My beard and body would be crawling with vermin again before we got back to the penitentiary.

Soon after my bath, an unfamiliar Japanese officer came to my cell. I was lying down, and while the bath ordeal had further sapped my little strength, it was also heartening to be a little cleaner, despite the fact that I once again was freezing. I cringed as he entered the cell, waiting for the kick or blow from his fist. When these didn't come, I shakily sat up. He stood, looking down at me and told me that he had notes with him from my trial at the Kempe

Tai. He spoke good English and said he wanted to ask me a few questions.

"You were found guilty of indiscriminate bombing of civilians," he told me, and then read aloud from the testimony. "We didn't care where the bombs fell," he quoted. "We were glad to kill the factory workers. If we killed them, the factories couldn't operate." He asked me if I had any comments. "That's not what I said," I explained. "and there wasn't any trial that I could see." He listened as I explained again, as I had in endless interrogations. "We wanted to hit the steel mill. We were not intentionally bombing civilians."

He asked more questions about the trial and my treatment at Kempe Tai. As he listened to me tell him about the beatings and tortures, his countenance changed. While he didn't seem shocked or surprised, he was clearly disturbed by what he heard. He seemed sincerely interested in learning the truth about what had occurred there. I found myself talking frankly with him at some length, telling him exactly what happened inside the Kempe Tai building. He wasn't exactly friendly—I was still his enemy—but his agitation at what he heard was obvious. I could tell he was a decent man.

Within a day or so, possibly even that day, as I lay on the floor of my cell, still unable to sit without effort, one of the guards stopped by and said in broken English, "You go hospital."

"Sure," I thought. "Unlikely." Still, I found myself encouraged. Maybe they really would take me to a hospital. The thought of a clean bed, decent food, medicine and nursing care was almost too much to wish for. After the bath and the interview, though, I couldn't help but grow hopeful at the guard's words. Maybe they weren't going to execute us after all.

Later, two guards came in, removed my kimono, put the hood on me and took me outside to a car. I was so relieved to be leaving that building. No matter where they might take me, at least I would be getting out of Kinoshu. I wondered about the others. Nearly six months had passed since we'd been thrown into that room and watched so carefully as we rotted away. Would the other three get to leave, too?

Shinagawa

"The fate of prisoners who fell sick was hardly better. Many a man who was sent to Shinagawa...simply went to his death. There was no sanitation; patients slept without blankets on flea-ridden mats. The operating tables were bare boards. When the hospital's crematorium was bombed to rubble, prisoners were forced to cremate the dead on spits over an open fire."

TIME, September 10, 1945

I was the only one they moved to Shinagawa. Designated as a hospital camp, Shinagawa had a little Red Cross medicine, primarily paregoric which was used to treat dysentery. Our physician was a fellow prisoner named Gottlieb, of the United States Navy. There were no nurses or clean beds. Still, it was here that I would regain the strength to sit up, to walk and, later, to work.

The camp was located in the suburbs between Tokyo and Yokohama. It consisted of a series of barracks, a warehouse, a guardhouse, and a headquarters building. A single ten-by-ten cell, which I would eventually inhabit, was attached to the guardhouse. The *benjo* occupied one corner of the compound, and a washstand, consisting of a wooden sink with cold running water, occupied another. A high wooden wall surrounded the camp. Designed to keep us in, this wall would prove to instrumental in saving our lives.

I arrived at Shinagawa in the afternoon of February 5, 1945, and was taken directly to one of the barracks where I was deposited onto one of the reedy mats like a limp sack of dirty laundry.

National Archives

A Japanese medic at the Shinagawa hospital camp for prisioners of war.

This large open room was laid out in what I would come to recognize as the standard configuration for prison barracks. The center of the room consisted of a bare dirt floor which extended in a rectangle to the door. Around this dirt area, which we referred to as the "rat pit", were wooden platforms, raised perhaps eighteen inches off the ground. These platforms provided a decking which extended to the walls of the room. Straw mats were laid out on the platforms. Crawling with lice, these mats were the only furnishings provided. When sitting up, you could either sit cross-legged on the mats or dangle your legs over the edge of the decking into the pit. There were no blankets in the unheated room and no quilted kimonos in sight.

There were probably forty other men in the room. They

seemed to be moving about freely and talking to one another at will. It was so strange to see people doing this. They were the first non-Asian faces I'd seen since I'd bailed out of the Reddy Teddy all those months before. The men were all obviously ill and starving, but to my eyes and ears, accustomed to dark, solitude and relative silence, the barracks was a bustling hub of activity. Those who caught my eye as I lay on the mat nodded to me or greeted me quietly. They were the best-looking group of people I'd ever seen.

Everyone there was aching for news about the war and the world outside. I was the first "new" prisoner they had seen in years, and even though I was extremely weak when I arrived, and my own information was six months old, they could hardly leave me alone for wanting to question me. Although I slept most of the time, if it looked at all like I was waking up and alert, someone nearby would begin to talk to me and a crowd would soon form. Their thirst for details was insatiable. They fired questions at me, absorbing my answers as quickly as possible before someone shouted out another. "What's going on in the war? Who's President? How do the people at home feel about the war?" They wanted details about the draft and rationing, and, of course, how well the New York Yankees were playing.

The presence of an American bomber pilot shot down over the Japanese homeland was incomprehensible to them. When these men had been captured, we were losing the war and it appeared that Japan would take everything. They had not seen or heard anything that would lead them to believe that the tide had turned.

They wanted to know about my capture, my previous captivity, and everything about B-29s and the bases in China. I was able to tell them that the Marianas had fallen before I was captured, and we all wondered about the progress of bases there. I think, more than anything, my presence gave them hope. I was physical proof that the war was advancing. Perhaps we would win. Perhaps we would go home.

I don't know how many days I lay inert on the mat, mostly sleeping. The infested mats were a continual nuisance. The hungry bedbugs chewed on me constantly. They were quick and about the size of a little fingernail. Sometimes, I'd reach up in my sleep to mash one that was gnawing on my ear, only to come more fully awake and realize that I had smashed five or six with a single blow. But while it was still disappointing to awaken each time and find myself still in Japan, it was a joy and relief to open my eyes and be out of Kinoshu and with these friendly men.

Even though I was weak, I did manage to get myself over to the rat pit for meals. The guards brought the food to the barracks in big buckets. Usually it was just rice or another grain I'd never seen before. Each of us had a small cup that we'd line up with the other cups on the edge of the rat pit. One of the prisoners distributed the portions into the cups. Because we were still on starvation diets, there was much bickering and talking about the size of the portions. The server had to be extremely careful that no prisoner got more food than any another. Every cup was eyed hungrily and jealously by all forty men. Sometimes we'd get soup, which was mainly water in which they'd boiled some weeds or even grass. Sometimes the soup had rice or grain in it. I was grateful to one of the other prisoners, an Englishman if I recall, who saw how I struggled with the chopsticks. He fashioned a crude spoon for me out of a scrap of tin he found somewhere, even going so far as to scratch my name onto it in Japanese.

At the beginning and end of each day, the prisoners were expected to gather at the rat pit to "stand *tenco*"—to be counted. If a prisoner was too weak to stand *tenco*, as I was when I first arrived, the highest-ranking prisoner in the barracks accounted for him as being *shushing*, asleep. Everyone else sat along the edge of the pit and counted off in Japanese. The counting was very fast, faster than seemed possible. If a prisoner didn't respond with the proper number fast enough, he was beaten. Apparently, the guards here at the hospital were as willing to beat a prisoner as those at any other camp.

Because I could hear the counting from where I lay, and because other prisoners were more than willing to coach me, I was able to learn to count in Japanese before I had to stand *tenco* myself. In situations where a prisoner stood *tenco* before he knew how to count in Japanese, the prisoners next to him would count ahead and whisper the proper response to him before his turn to speak.

The other prisoners taught me another valuable skill. They taught me a way to kill lice. The lice were about the size of a grain of rice and hid in the seams of our clothing. By taking off our clothes and turning them inside out, we could work both thumbnails down the outsides of the seams, squishing the lice in between. Because the lice laid eggs by the millions and there was always a new generation ready to hatch, I'm not sure this procedure made a significant difference in actual lice populations. But the psychological effect of killing hundreds of lice in just a few minutes of concentrated effort made the process worthwhile. It was one of the chief occupations of our day. I began to obsess about designing new seamless military uniforms, so that when Americans were taken prisoner in the future, there would be no place for the lice to hide and multiply. This idea captured my imagination so fully, and I was so convinced of the necessity of it, that my intention for the remainder of my time in Japan was to return home and develop these seam-free uniforms.

Dr. Gottlieb told us that each of us was supposed to be getting regular packages from the Red Cross containing food, vitamins, soap and other items. We could see the Red Cross boxes stacked to the ceiling in the guard house. Although I was issued V-Mail forms twice at Shinagawa to write short notes to my wife,

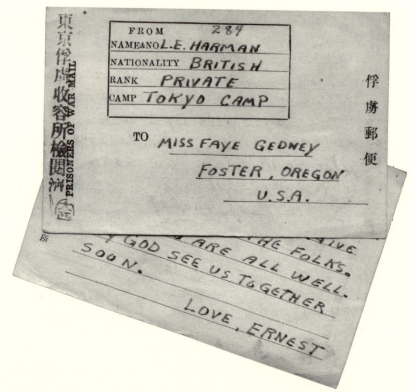

FROM 289
NAME&NO *L.E. HARMAN*
NATIONALITY *BRITISH*
RANK *PRIVATE*
CAMP *TOKYO CAMP*

TO *MISS FAYE GEDNEY*
FOSTER, OREGON
U.S.A.

...RE ALL WELL.
SOON. *GOD SEE US TOGETHER*
LOVE, ERNEST

V-Mail messages sent by Ernest Pickett to his wife, Faye, during his stay at Shinagawa. He used a British soldier's name and rank on one, hoping it would get past censors if his own did not. The messages were delivered after the end of the war.

I didn't get a single Red Cross box or receive any mail while in Japan. Gottlieb said that the guards were using the Red Cross boxes themselves and probably getting rich selling what they didn't use. Faye eventually received the V-Mail letters—a couple of months after my liberation. Other than that, the only benefit I can recall receiving from the Red Cross boxes that should have been mine, was possibly a small piece of soap.

I'm not sure that my soap came from the Red Cross, but somehow I had a little bit for awhile and I treasured it. One day, I was out by the washstand when a guard saw my soap and offered to trade it for a dried squid he had. It was an easy trade. I jumped at it. The squid had been pounded out to a diameter of five to six inches, and was about a quarter of an inch thick. Both sides of it were coated with gray mold. I wanted, needed, to eat it. All of it. I started with the legs and tentacles. It was like chewing rubber.

I worked at each bite, chewing as much as I could before swallowing. Another prisoner came over, wanting to know what I had. Afraid he would take it from me or make me share it, I told him it was a dried rat and he went away. I ate it all.

The combination of medicine and the improvement over conditions at Kinoshu went a long way toward restoring my strength. Being outside, having contact with fellow prisoners, and having freedom to sit or lie down as I wished all had a restorative effect.

Although by no means well, I improved enough to enjoy interacting with those around me. Most of the inmates were American, but there were also Canadian, British, and Australian prisoners. The other prisoners I met at Shinagawa had already been imprisoned for three or four years. Many of them had been taken on Corregidor, Bataan, or on the Malay Peninsula and had been transported to Japan in the holds of Japanese cargo ships. These ships became known as Hell Ships as a result of the extreme conditions that prevailed during the journey. Many prisoners didn't survive the ordeal. Those who did reach Japan were put to work as slave labor in mines or factories or as longshoremen.

Two marines I met there, Meyers and Hetgar, had been captured in China on the riverboat Panay before the war began, and had been working in copper mines. Bathed in sweat, both from labor and from the extreme temperatures underground, they were brought up each night into the freezing cold of the Japanese winter. Given no clothing or protection from the cold, they eventually contracted pneumonia and were sent to Shinagawa.

The majority of prisoners were military personnel, but there were also a few civilians captured on Wake Island and elsewhere. One man, "Pop" Barger, had been a civilian, working for Morrison-Knutson, contractors, on Wake. He was a husky, burly man who was probably between thirty and forty years old. Another civilian who especially befriended me was the British Port Commissioner of Hong Kong, Jock McDonald. Jock was a character, dispatching his special brand of humor with a thick Scottish accent. He filled me in on the cumshaw racket. Smuggling had been rampant in his jurisdiction and the smugglers and the police had enjoyed a profitable understanding. When the smugglers brought their junks into port, loaded with contraband, they would leave a little of the illegal merchandise where the police could find it, thereby allowing the police to save face while taking a hefty percentage for overlooking the rest. This payment was called cumshaw, and it had made Jock a wealthy man. He had enjoyed a privileged status in Hong Kong, with a fine house, servants, and lots of money. He was captured when Hong Kong fell to the Japanese and had no idea what had happened to his wife. Because she was Chinese, he feared the worst.

Each inmate had his own tales of horror. One of the men at the hospital had witnessed the executions of prisoners at a previous camp. In listening to him relate what he saw, I learned what my own fate would have been had my execution been carried out at Kinoshu. The prisoners had been made to dig their own graves, or trenches, and then kneel at the edge, facing the hole. Using a huge samurai sword, one of the soldiers stood behind them, swung the sword, and beheaded them. The heads fell into the graves and the bodies were kicked in after. As far as I knew, my death sentence was still in effect or could be reinstated at any time. Deep down, I still didn't expect to get out of Japan alive and these images of beheading were haunting. They added to the constant fear and wariness that was part of my existence. Being moved from Kinoshu had given me a small glimmer of hope, and events at Shinagawa would provide yet another. But still, there were so many ways to die.

Shortly after midnight on the morning of March 10, 1945, we awoke to the sound of air raid sirens and the drone of heavy aircraft overhead. The noise, even in the barracks, was deafening. The boom of antiaircraft fire, the explosions of bombs, and the sound of pandemonium in the streets all added to the roar. Within five minutes the room was lit from the outside as if it were midday. An incendiary raid! The city was on fire.

Guards, manic and frightened, ran into the barracks, ordering us outside. Their hate for us boiled in their eyes, but they couldn't kill us. They needed us to fight the fire. Shouting, they rushed us out to the yard and herded us toward the gate. Our senses were bombarded with the noise and smoke and confusion. Low-flying B-29s passed overhead. They were massive. Although the fires already made it so light that we could see the planes clearly, the searchlights around the city continued their constant prowl. When a light passed across the belly of a plane, the huge aircraft gleamed like polished silver.

Oh, they were big. And terrible in their destruction. They flew over at about five thousand feet, bomb bays open. We could watch them bombing to the north of us. Instead of flying in formation, they made individual bomb runs, spread out across the city. Each bomb fell as a huge ball of fire dropping from the belly of the plane. Halfway to the ground it exploded, spreading a blanket of what I assumed to be burning phosphorous. As the phosphorous dropped, it sparkled like an enormous inverted Christmas tree, perhaps a half mile wide, hanging in the sky.

The thin lumber and paper of the Japanese buildings served as tinder to a match. Once the rain of burning material fell on a structure, it was a matter of a few minutes before the building was engulfed. Watching from a distance, it seemed almost instantaneous.

The phosphorus hit and whole blocks of the city ignited in flame.

I was certain we were going to die. The guards were irrational. As they herded us through the gate and out into the city, they were screaming, frenzied. Faces contorted and sweating, it seemed as if they were looking for any excuse to bayonet us. And then there was the threat of the bombs. Our camp was unmarked. There was no reason to think that we wouldn't be blanketed by the next sweep of the city. I knew that even a drop of phosphorous would be deadly, that it would burn through steel. I could only imagine what it would do to flesh. We watched every plane that passed overhead, looking to see if it was the one that would kill us.

The fire was an inferno. We could see the silhouettes of people running through the streets in the distance. The heat was incredible, almost too hot to breathe. Smoke and cinders blew in swirls around us, the heat from the fire creating a wind of its own. Prodded to the edge of the blaze, we were put on hand pumps. Seeing these old-fashioned pumps, I was reminded of pictures I had seen of firefighting from the last century. The pumps consisted of a tall central cylinder from which two large opposing arms extended. At the end of the arms, and perpendicular to them, were long bars at which we stood, four or five abreast, and pumped, much as if we were propelling a railroad handcar.

Sick and weak, we pumped with everything we had, although in our weakened conditions it couldn't have been too effective. The crazed guards pressed in close, screaming, bayonets at the ready. We knew that if we slacked off a bit, we would be dead. Fighting the fire was futile. It was burning out of control. With hardly any water pressure and inadequate equipment, there was no way we would stop the blaze. After we had pumped for what seemed an eternity, we were allowed to drop off, one at a time, to spell one another. While we were on a pump, however, we knew we had to work.

Work or die.

The raid probably lasted a couple of hours. By the time the planes were gone, there were no sirens left in the city to sound the all-clear. We continued to fight the flames until just before daylight. The camp, miraculously, was untouched. The wind must have been blowing in our favor, carrying sparks away from the camp, or at least not over the high wall. I had been so sure we would die that night. Between the bombs and the fire and the guards, it had seemed that there was no way to survive. My fear had been overwhelming. And then it was over. We were dismissed to the barracks where we sank to our mats, exhausted, and slept.

The fire had burned up to the street that ran in front of the camp. There is no doubt that without the wall, the camp would have been consumed as well. It was now an island, surrounded by miles of charred desolation. There was no color or life left within eyesight. Everything was ashes. Only the charred spikes of chimneys and the burned-out shells of concrete buildings attested to the previous existence of a city in what was now a smoldering desert. Lathes and other machines the civilians had used in their homes to crank out weapons and equipment stood stubbornly in the ashes of houses, as if mimicking the Army's determination to fight to the death. Here and there, the carcass of a horse rested in the streets, roasted. We had one meal of horsemeat and bone marrow following the fire. Aside from tiny bits of fish and the moldy squid, it was the only meat I had in Japan.

According to various accounts, somewhere between eighty-four and one hundred and thirty thousand people were incinerated in that raid on Tokyo. Although we had no way of knowing at the time, the raid on Tokyo was the first of five incendiary raids on Japan occurring in a ten-day period. The cities of Nagoya, Osaka, and Kobe would share the same fate as Tokyo, with Nagoya being hit twice.

National Archives

Aerial photograph showing a burned-out section of Tokyo. In the fourteen weeks that began with the March 10, 1945 fire raid on Tokoyo, B-29 bombing missions wiped out more than 100 square miles of Japan's six most important cities. To save civilian lives, the B-29s began dropping warning leaflets in advance of the attacks, advising the populations to evacuate. By the end of the war, 60 of Japan's urban centers were destroyed. Apart from Kyoto, which was not a target due to its cultural and historical importance, only Hiroshima, Nagasaki, Niigata, and Kokura—barred from the B-29 target lists in anticipation of the readiness of the atomic bomb—remained untouched.

Although one might expect that the death of so many people around us might arouse compassion in us, the brutality we had all suffered at the hands of the Japanese left little room for sympathy in our hearts. The disregard for human life and the horrors each of us had seen and endured up to this point translated for most of us into a hatred of all Japanese. All we knew, or could think about in terms of the raid, was that we had survived, and, considering that there was nothing left to bomb in our vicinity, we might hope to stay out of the path of future U.S. actions. Outside of that, we were afraid of the guards and we worried about food.

Even if more humanitarian thoughts had filtered into our consciousness as a result of the fire, they had no chance to take root, for our hate was immediately fanned by events resulting from that blaze. During the commotion of the fire, two of the prisoners, one British, one Australian, decided to take advantage of the confusion and help themselves to some bread from the warehouse. They managed to come away with one precious, life-giving loaf apiece. But, they were caught on the way back to the barracks. Beaten mercilessly, the morning found them hanging by their thumbs near the gate.

Although the two were in plain sight, we didn't dare go near them. The guards took bowls of rice to them at mealtimes, making a big display of showing it to the men and then placing it on the ground where they could see it. No food, no water, exposed to the elements, and in incredible pain, their suffering must have been unimaginable.

I didn't see them die, because soon after the March 10 raid, I was moved to the cell attached to the guard house. Apparently, the Japanese had second thoughts about my interaction with the other prisoners. I spent more time in solitary confinement in this cell than I spent with the other prisoners in the barracks. This term of solitary, however, was much more liberal than my previous confinement had been. I could move around the cell freely and could look out a window at the activity in the prison yard.

Unlike my cell at Kinoshu, though, my solitary cell at Shinagawa had no *benjo*. To go to the bathroom, I had to knock on the door that joined my cell to the guard house and ask the guards for permission to go. A pair of them would escort me to the latrine building about one hundred feet away. At this point, I was still weak and could barely walk and, suffering from dysentery, the trips to the *benjo* were necessarily frequent. One night I had an especially pressing need. I called the guards who, for some reason made me walk clear into the guardhouse with them and through their long barracks to the outside door on the far end. They were supposed to come with me, but instead instructed me to go ahead. I went outside, walking back alongside the building toward the latrine which lay beyond my cell at the end of the building. But I couldn't hold my bowels that far. With no other alternative unless I wanted to soil myself, I stopped, dropped my pants, and let go. My guards came around the corner after me about that time and were furious when they saw the mess I had made. They beat me so severely I could hardly crawl back to the cell.

In a way, the psychological effect of such beatings was almost worse than the injuries that resulted from them, although to be so beat up, with all the pain and sores on top of illness was bad enough. But those guards must have known that I had no control over the dysentery. It was they who had delayed things by making me take the long way around. What would they have had me do? They were inhuman and cruel. My fear was consuming, but my hatred knew no bounds.

The guards at Shinagawa had the big heavy wooden swords I had so suffered from at the Kempe Tei headquarters. They practiced with them for hours in the prison yard, sparring with furious intent. I knew how much it hurt to be walloped with those awful swords, yet the guards held them with two hands, swinging them with full power and speed at their opponents, hitting hard whenever possible. These were clearly serious engagements, and the blows they delivered were crushing. Yet, the matches continued day after day, seemingly at every opportunity. I couldn't understand what motivated the guards to participate in these vicious battles.

I was probably at Shinagawa for two-and-a-half months before the guards came for me again, basket hood in hand. I had begun to believe that my death sentence had been lifted. "It wouldn't make sense for them to send me to a hospital just to execute me later," I reasoned. But the appearance of the guards, there to take me away, stunned me. As they tied my hands and put me into a car, I was numb. I didn't want to go. Wherever they took me, it had to be worse than Shinagawa. After all, this was supposed to be a hospital and I was far from well.

The Americans bombing Tokyo in force meant that an end to the war might be possible, but my getting out of Japan alive wasn't an idea I could really grasp. Too much could happen.

Omori

"A friend loveth at all times, and a brother is born for adversity."
Proverbs 17:17

As the car that carried me from Shinagawa wormed its way through Tokyo traffic, I prayed that I wasn't headed back to Kinoshu, or, Dear God, not Kempe Tai. Yet I had no reason to believe I could be going anywhere better. The uncertainty of not knowing what was going to happen next was a torture of its own. Where was I going? And what would they do to me there? Wherever I was going, I could be sure I was in for more beatings and more starvation.

I was still too weak to do much but slump in my seat, waiting with resignation for whatever they chose to do to me next. Only the energy of my hate gave me strength to hold my head up as we drove. They wouldn't see me shaking or know how afraid I really was.

After an hour or more, the car pulled to a stop and my two guards and I got out. It was ominously quiet. No city noise. I was so conditioned to anticipate danger every time something new occurred that the stillness could only mean that something terrifying was about to happen. In fear, my senses closed into narrow focus; I breathed rapidly under my hood, glimpsing small patches of yellow dirt at my feet.

With a guard gripping each arm, we started walking, soon stepping up onto a wooden surface. I could hear our hollow footsteps and decided we were on some kind of bridge. I was totally at their mercy, as always. It seemed as if we walked forever. Why such a long bridge? Over what? And worse, what was on the other side?

After five hundred feet or so, we finally reached the other end of the bridge. I heard other Japanese guards converse briefly with my escorts who, without breaking stride, propelled me forward. After another few yards, we stopped briefly, and I could tell we were entering a building.

As we entered the room, the guards pulled off my hood. We were in a long, wooden barracks, constructed of the same rough lightweight lumber I'd seen everywhere. There was barely enough light to make out the rat pit that ran in a line from the front door straight down the middle of the room to another door. The smell was nauseating. There were scraggly, starving Americans lying on straw-matted platforms on either side of the aisle. They eyed me silently as the guards steered me toward the second doorway.

The view in the second room was much the same. The rat pit ran to the end of the dark, foul room. Again, straw-matted platforms extended to the walls. And as in the other room, there were bearded, lice-infested men lying or sitting on the platforms. I didn't have a chance to take in much more of my surroundings, though, for as I came to a stop in the doorway of the room, a shout went up. I gasped in disbelief at what I saw. Suddenly, a new life pulsed in my veins. My crew!

The guys jumped to their feet and crowded around me, all talking at once. I didn't even notice when my escorts released me and left. "My God, Pickett, you look like hell." "We were sure you were dead. Where have you been?" I was so happy to see them. I made a mental count: Humphrey, Rewitz, Kennard, Bishop, Armstrong and Kazarian. They looked roughed up and hungry, but they were alive! My chest tightened and tears sprang to my eyes.

I noticed other men coming forward, too. I guessed that there were thirty to forty men in the room altogether. Three of them seemed especially happy to see me, which seemed strange, since I didn't recognize them.

One, of them, a tall blond, maybe six-foot-two or six-foot-three, approached me and extended his hand. "Pickett, I'm Colonel Richard Carmichael. I really missed your fine dinners after you left Kinoshu. We don't eat dinner here." Carmichael! A man I'd known for months, but had never seen. Despite the sagging skin and filth that covered him, I could tell that Carmichael was a handsome well-built man. Very military in bearing, but smiling broadly. I was practically speechless, unable to believe what was happening.

Another voice piped up. "When they hauled you out of there, we figured you were dead." There was no mistaking the East Coast accent. This one was Irving Newman. Newman was smaller than I with a wide mouth and medium complexion. Harold Mann was there, too. Six feet tall, dark eyes and black hair. The three men who had sustained me and helped me hold on to my small scraps of humanity during all those months of solitary confinement were there in the flesh, standing before me. It was strange to see what they looked like after having heard their voices for so many months, yet they seemed liked long-lost brothers.

I wanted to hold on to these men, all of them, and not let go. There was hope, there was life. I'd known some of these men long before this terrible nightmare had begun and it was profoundly moving to see them again. That former life which sometimes seemed so distant had been real, and seeing these men made it more real again. While I knew I could still die in Japan, and probably would, for this time at least, I was with friends.

I must have been a mess as I walked in there, for as hollow-cheeked and gaunt as that group looked to me, wearing the remnants of the uniforms in which they were captured, they behaved as though I looked much worse. As soon as the initial greetings were over, they hurried to get me onto the platform and sitting down. "Easy with him," I heard someone say. "He looks pretty sick," I heard another.

In truth, I was happy to sit. I'd probably walked a thousand feet since I'd left the car, and the hike had sapped what little strength I had. I needed to lie down, but how could I? I wanted to drink in the sight of these men and listen to them talk to me—about anything.

I had noticed right away that there were some faces missing, and of course I wanted to know about the missing men. I had seen Roberts' body that first night and knew he was dead, but his absence was still painful, a reminder that I wasn't waking up from what I wished so much was just a bad dream. There was no news of Nixon or Henry. It was possible they'd ridden the plane down. They could have been hit, passed out, or gotten stuck. Armstrong, Bishop and Humphrey had been in the rear control compartment and had barely made it out of the plane. Humphrey had seen Bishop moving around near the hatch, but he wasn't jumping. Later, when Bishop couldn't recall leaving the plane, they realized that they had been running out of oxygen in the depressurized plane and probably would have passed out without jumping had Humphrey not pushed Bishop out with his foot and then grabbed Armstrong and done the same. Humphrey reported that after he'd pushed the other two out, he paused long enough to notice that the plane was still flying level. He briefly entertained the idea of going back to the intercom to double-check the bailout order, but decided since he'd kicked the other two out, he'd better go with them.

Humphrey had gone last of the three, but his seat pack had gotten hung up on the door frame, and he was stuck, halfway out of the plane. He remembered looking over at the number three engine as he hung there and seeing smoke pouring out of it. Fortunately, after taking a beating on the shins by the hatch door, he was able to twist himself free and drop into a flat spin.

There was simply no way of knowing about Nixon or Henry. Everything had happened so fast, and in the mayhem after the initial blast, we wouldn't have even known if the tail section had been hit. If Nixon and Henry did make it out of the plane, they must have been killed in the chute or died in captivity. We had little hope that they were still alive.

But what about Robins, our navigator? In the heat and smoke and confusion in the cockpit, I had felt certain that he was there, ready to bail out. Did he run out of oxygen in the smoke and pass out before he could jump, or did he ride the plane down? It was likely that he had bailed out and been killed on the ground, but nobody had seen or heard anything of him since the blast in the cockpit. I was terribly upset by this news. Maybe he had been hit and never left his station, and in the confusion and thick smoke I had just thought I'd seen him.

While intellectually I knew that had Kennard and I not jumped quickly into the wheel well to force that little opening for escape, we would have all been dead in moments, this being unable to account for Robins, whom I had believed was ready to jump when I left the plane, created a nightmare that would haunt my dreams and many waking hours for the rest of my life. Had I seen what I had thought I'd seen? Did he get out of the plane, or didn't he? It would always be a question for me, impossible to answer.

After the initial reunion, there was a lot of catching up to do. The fellas introduced me to the rest of the men in our barracks. There were thirty-six of us all together, all from B-29 crews. Everyone had received some variation of the "Special Prisoner" treatment I had seen. Apparently, the Japanese still kept the B-29, *B-Nijukyu* prisoners segregated from the other prisoners. I never figured out why that separation was important, but I suspected it was because they hated us most for bringing the war to the Japanese homeland. If they had us grouped together, it would be easier to kill us all when the time came.

One by one, I was able to learn from the men of my crew what had happened to them after we'd been shot down. The enlisted men had all been sent to a labor camp at an Army base. Humphrey, indeed, had been at Kempe Tai headquarters when Kennard and I were there and had been held in that hell hole for many months. Kennard's arm had never received any medical attention, and had eventually crusted over and formed a heavy, red scar tissue that covered the two inch gap down to his bone. He had no use of his lower limb and his hand had begun to shrivel. That he survived the wound was a miracle.

Rewitz had a uniquely terrifying tale to tell. He had been put on a ship and taken to a small village in China, where he was put on display beside a street in a bamboo cage alongside three American fighter pilots. One day, the Japanese tied ropes around the other prisoners and took them out into the middle of the street, where a crowd had gathered. The soldiers poured gasoline on the men, set them on fire, and dragged them through the streets. Rewitz could only watch helplessly, figuring that he was next. In the typically confounding and random style of handling prisoners, the Japanese soon after put Rewitz on a plane and sent him back to Japan, where he ended up at Omori.

Rewitz wasn't the only prisoner put on display. One of the other B-29 crewmen at Omori was Hap Halloran. Hap was a good-natured, warm-hearted, fun-loving kid who had been taken, soon after his capture early in 1945, to the Tokyo zoo. There he had been stripped of his clothing and put, naked, on display in one of the animal cages. There was no place to hide, no clothing or blankets to protect him from the elements, and his food was dirty. People filed by and stared at him throughout the day. There was never a moment of privacy. At night he sat in the cold and listened to the animals in the other parts of the zoo. Again, the Japanese, seemingly on a whim, soon changed their minds and moved him to Omori.

In talking more with Kennard, I learned more about how Bud Roberts died the night we were shot down. Kennard and Roberts had landed near one another. Roberts' foot, which had been nearly blown off in the cockpit blast, was hanging to his leg by just a few tendons. For sport, the Japanese soldiers had tied his leg to a long stick and dragged him through the streets. Kennard said that the tendons in Robert's leg stretched out as he was dragged until they were a couple of feet long. When the Japanese tired of the game, one of the soldiers used his Samurai and in one blow severed the tendons. Bud bled to death shortly thereafter.

The horror stories were many. I was happy to have escaped one of the interrogation techniques I heard about at Omori. One interrogator had hooked up a hose. When he wanted to punish a prisoner, the guards forced the water hose down the prisoner's throat and turned the water on. To avoid drowning, the prisoner had no choice but to swallow the water as quickly as he could. Aside from the immediate panic of gagging and trying not to drown, the pain of the overextended stomach, distended to hideous proportions, had been overwhelming.

There was some good news in all this, however. Bishop reported that he had shot down a Zero over the target just before we were hit. At least we'd taken someone with us. Of course, we didn't know it then, but Bishop's hit was never recorded in the mission log. The newer prisoners gave us updates on the progress of the war. The massive B-29 operations now being launched from the Marianas were reducing the Japanese cities to ashes. We had virtually eliminated shipping and their war production was crippled enough to be nonexistent. It was puzzling as to why the Japanese even continued the war. We knew about their code of honor, *bushido*, and knew that they were honor-bound to fight to the death, to fight for the Emperor. But we prisoners had seen no honor in the Japanese. With rare exception, we had seen only brutality and sadism.

Even with our hate of all people and things Japanese, we were still able to distinguish personalities in our guards. At Omori, there was one guard, Watanabe, who we viewed as a Good Guard. He spoke fluent English and had been to the United States before the war began and wanted to start an import/export business when the war was over. He tried to be friendly to us, and though it was hard to actually like a Japanese, Watanabe made it possible. He was a decent, fine man. I don't believe he ever beat anyone. We all respected and appreciated him. We could often hear arguments in the guard house between Watanabe and other guards. We were certain that he was angered by the atrocities he witnessed.

The other two guards who spent the most time with our group of thirty-six prisoners were animals. They looked for excuses to smash a rifle butt into someone's face. Once they began, their beatings were thorough and there was nothing we could do for a victim but stand and watch and hope he would get up when the beating was over. We nicknamed the worst guard Horseface. He was an ugly, sadistic brute, who I believe was tried as a war criminal after the war and might have been hanged. I've always hoped that he was.

We were careful to address this guard as Horseface as though the name were a title of great respect. If Watanabe knew what the name meant, he must not have given us away, because Horseface always seemed a little pleased with the special name.

Sometimes small ways of independence can mean so much.

Of Beans and Goldfish

"A friend is someone who knows the song in your heart, and can sing it back to you even when you have forgotten the words."

Unknown

The camp at Omori was built on an island in Tokyo Bay, across the long wooden footbridge from the township of Omori. It was hard for us to know how many prisoners were there because our group of Special Prisoners was kept carefully isolated from everyone else. There were no trees or vegetation to speak of, just packed dirt and the long low wooden barracks. We never saw men from any of the other barracks in the prison yard, so I assumed that any other prisoners at Omori were confined to their barracks. We were confined to barracks, too, except when we went out to the *benjo*, or were marched out to work. To my knowledge, the B-29 prisoners were the only ones in the camp that worked.

There was a washstand of sorts and a *benjo* house. To say this, though, implies that there was some kind of bathroom facility for the camp. In reality, the washstand was a wooden trough with a trickle of cold water running through it from a standing pipe faucet. There was no soap, and the only way to dry your hands was to wipe them on your filthy uniform. The *benjo* consisted of a wooden building that covered a long pit dug out of the dirt. The pit was roughly three feet deep with a small stream of water running through it from one end of the building to the other. Along the edge of the pit was a long wooden bench on which to sit for bowel movements, back end suspended over the trench. There was nothing to use for toilet paper, and no way to clean ourselves. Those with amebic dysentery, such as I, spent many hours on the uncomfortable perch over those trenches, adding to the foul layers of filth already caked on our bodies.

The only nice thing about the *benjo* at Omori was that we could use it any time, just by asking the ever-present guard in the barracks for permission. Of course, we couldn't stop to chat in the front barracks, or deviate from course once we were in the yard, but it was refreshing to have this tiny bit of freedom to walk to the *benjo* unescorted and to use the cold water washstand to splash a little water on our bodies and to rinse our hands.

There was a ten-foot-high wooden fence around the perimeter of the camp, but because our work details took us out of the camp, we had the opportunity to see what lay on the other side of the wall. Tokyo Bay was enormous. I could see Japanese warships anchored across the water, miles away. The city of Tokyo and its suburbs ranged around the edges of the bay. The fence around the camp seemed superfluous. Even if someone had been able to swim the great distance, there would be no place for a Caucasian to hide once he reached the mainland.

While we were not allowed to mix with the group who occupied the front half of our barracks, we were able to maintain some acquaintance with them. The two sections of the barracks were separated by a wall, but we could sometimes carry on short conversations through the barrier, and we could nod in greeting as we walked through their area to go to the latrine or were marched out on work detail.

There were thirty-some men in this group, too. It seemed to be made up of Marines and Navy personnel. Among them was Pappy Boyington, the fighter ace who led the famous Black Sheep squadron. He had been on a mission off the Malay Peninsula when he got hit and had to ditch. His wingman stayed with him until he was down, and then, having marked his position, left. Soon after Boyington hit the water, a Japanese submarine surfaced and took him prisoner. Boyington was a strutting, cocky sort. Even in the leveling degradation of our situation, there was a boastful, "I'm a big shot" quality about him that I didn't like.

Another famous prisoner on the other side of the wall was Commander O'Kane of the submarine Tang. O'Kane was a mild-mannered, pleasant man who had sunk more Japanese ships than any other submarine commander in the war. He was directly responsible for many of the heavy losses suffered by the Japanese during their evacuation of the Philippines. On one cruise alone, he sank sixteen Japanese ships, becoming ever bolder and daring as they neared Japan. "I just followed them all the way up to Tokyo," he said. His submarine was sunk by one of his own torpedoes when it boomeranged in shallow water.

I liked O'Kane very much and had a lot of respect for him.

While everyone was suffering from starvation and disease, there were some cases in the other group in our barracks that made the rest of us feel grateful for what health we had. One of their fighter pilots, a young blond man, probably no more than nineteen or twenty, had a broken ankle which had never been set. With no crutch, he hobbled around on the stump of his leg with his foot dangling to the side at a sickening angle. Why couldn't the Japanese have helped him even a little bit?

One night, a sailor on the other side of the barracks got extremely sick and was in tremendous pain. We could hear his agonized cries clearly through the wall. As the night wore on, we learned that a medic or doctor in the group had determined that his intestine or some other internal organ had ruptured and that his only hope for survival was surgery. With no anesthetic or sterile equipment, they operated on him with a razor blade. It must have taken their entire group to hold him down. We could hear his piercing screams for what seemed like hours. "Help me. Someone help me," the sailor begged. On our side of the barracks we could only sit in nail-biting stillness, or pace, listening as the relentless horror waged on in the other room. Unaccountably, the sailor survived.

I soon fell into the daily routine with the other men. At first, when the guards marched the men out to work, I was told to remain behind. I was still very sick and extremely weak, suffering from dysentery, wet and dry beriberi, and of course, malnutrition. To sit and wait alone in the dismal barracks, though, while my friends were elsewhere, was unbearable. I should have been resting, but I much preferred the idea of working with the other men. Within two or three days, I volunteered for the work detail.

We stood *tenco* every night and every morning as we had in the barracks at Shinagawa. By now, everyone knew how to count in Japanese and we raced through our head count with blinding speed. The twice-daily meals were as important at Omori as they had been in Shinagawa, too, and it was of utmost importance to every man that the portions were equal.

They had all held elections before I arrived, and Dick Bishop had been elected as rice dipper. By the time I got to Omori, though, there was no more rice. Instead, they gave us a grain which they called *corion.* To me, it looked and tasted like boiled corn tassels.

At every meal, the prisoners lined their little bamboo cups along the edge of the decking while Bishop stood in the rat pit, carefully dipping into the bucket and putting portions into the cup. No spilled kernel went uneaten, despite the filthy conditions. Only someone who was starving could fully understand the important responsibility held by the rice dipper. His was a position of trust and high esteem, and the pressure on him was tremendous.

We also had soup at Omori. Sometimes the soup was just a bucket of warm water with a fish head floating in it. Other times, there might have been some greens or grass thrown into it. Often, if there was anything leafy at all in the water, it had thorns on it. There was never any evidence of meat in the bucket and the water could certainly not be considered a broth. Still, every drop of it was precious and we chewed our corn-tassel-like grain purposely, trying to get every bit of the scant nutritional value possible.

A couple of times, we were given enormous unwashed daikon. These had been grown in human excrement and we had no means to wash them. As we divided the filthy, tasteless root, wiping our hands on our soiled clothing, it was a terrible choice as to whether to eat our share or to bypass the much-needed nourishment.

Shortly after my arrival, I was elected soup dipper. For the rest of our internment, Bishop and I worked side-by-side each meal, dripping precious life into tiny cups while our companions watched hungrily.

I've been told that when I first arrived at Omori, the men were so concerned for my health that they gave me a slightly larger portion, which meant less food for each of them. I was still too sick to even notice. That these starving men would sacrifice some of their own much-needed food for me is a testament to the kind of people they were. I do recall in the first days, however, receiving a rice paste that the other men didn't get. It was called rice *colly*, or something quite close. But even that was not something I spent much time thinking about. I just ate it.

We were lucky in our barracks to have two fine men as superior officers. The Japanese appointed them as barracks leaders. If someone in the barracks stepped out of line in a guard's view, the barracks leaders were held responsible. One, Colonel Richard King, was a group commander. I believe he had been at West Point. The other was my friend from Kinoshu, Dick Carmichael. Before joining the B-29 program, Carmichael had fought in the East from the Philippines all the way down the Malay Peninsula. He

National Archives

Richard Carmichael

had been a group commander at Great Bend. Both King and Carmichael were fair-minded and behaved as gentlemen. Thanks to their leadership and example, we didn't have many problems between the men in our barracks. It seems that thirty-six men in close quarters under extreme stress might have some difficulties over time, but any flare-ups in our group were minor and were dispelled quickly. One might assume that everyone was simply too weak to get angry, which might have been part of it, but I also believe that we had a group of quality men who respected our senior officers. The group had a strong bond. All part of the original B-29 program, we were in this mess together.

There wasn't a lot to do in the barracks. Sometimes, men would talk about home: share a story, or remark on how nice it would be to have this or to do this or that. For the most part, though, we were talked out. The body's drawing in of the mind as a response to starvation was at work on us all. We sat long hours, sitting or lying silently, sometimes napping or smashing the bedbugs that came within easy reach. The seam-squashing lice destruction technique I'd first seen at Shinagawa was a daily ritual for us all. It was a serious job, one in which we engaged with methodical intensity. But after killing lice and bedbugs, there wasn't much to do.

One can't say that we really lived in those spare wooden barracks. It's more that we just didn't die. The camp was nothing more than a warehouse for strong young men whose bodies had become shells for stubbornly beating hearts, and hosts for disease and parasites. We conserved what energy we could while our minds retreated into a starvation haze for long periods of each day and night.

While there was always a guard present, there wasn't much for him to do. He was probably more bored than we were. At least we could talk to someone if we wanted. We certainly weren't interested in doing anything to get the guard excited. A still guard was a good guard.

We didn't sit in our stupor all day, though. At some point, early or late, according to the guard's whim, we were ordered out to the work detail. Some days we worked long hours, some days short. There didn't seem to be a strict schedule except that we worked every day. It was spring when I arrived at Omori, and the Japanese had us planting and tending a vast garden which they established in the burned-out village.

Each day, we lined up single file, in no particular order, and were marched out of the camp and over the long wooden bridge that connected our island to the city. The bridge couldn't have been more than eight feet wide, if that, but it was at least five hundred feet long. It was such a long tramp over that bridge. While the work details were difficult for me physically, it was always a relief to get out of the oppressive dark barracks and away from the camp. We had more freedom of movement and conversation outside, or at least it felt so.

The village of Omori had been burned out by previous incendiary bombing raids and consisted primarily of a grid of paved streets connecting endless city blocks of gray and black rubble. From the crown of the bridge, you could see for miles as the desolation fanned out to the distance. Little vegetation had survived the conflagrations and only a charred tree trunk stood out here and there to attest that there had once been green in the landscape.

Because there was no place for us to hide or run to, there was usually only one guard with us. We knew our jobs and were expected to work constantly. Even though we might be spread out over a wide area, sometimes out of sight of the guard, we all kept to task. We knew the consequence of a guard being even a little displeased. The beatings for offenses, suspected or real, were certain and severe, although as time passed, the beatings subsided, and only Horseface remained a constant threat.

The Japanese were eager for us to raise as much food as possible in this scorched earth, and as some men cleared debris or spaded and dug shallow ditches, others were sent out into the neighborhoods to bring in fertilizer. This fertilizer could be found in abundance, for every burned out house had had a *benjo* box, and all we had to do was go through the neighborhoods and collect the abandoned human waste, take it back to the gardens, and ladle it into the furrows.

Carmichael and I were assigned as a team to collect fertilizer. We were given a large wooden vat, which was suspended by rope on a long pole. I'm guessing the vat held between five and ten gallons of waste. With one man in front of the vat, and one in back, we could lift the vat and carry it by placing the pole on one shoulder and walking in single file. I always walked in front, scouting out burned foundations and locating the *benjo*. When we found one, we eased the vat down, fished the *benjo* box out of the foundation, and using a long-handled dipper, ladled its contents into the vat. It was a smelly, gut-twisting job; one that never got less repugnant.

We called our vats honey buckets, and those who filled and carried the vile tubs to and from the gardens were the Honey Bucket Brigade. Carmichael and I got to be good friends during these forays in search of *benjo* boxes. He had a great sense of humor, and out of earshot of the guards, we could talk about anything that interested us.

One day, as we were picking our way through debris, I heard Carmichael's voice pipe up behind me.

"You know, Pickett, I outrank you. From here on, I think I'll pack the front end of the honey bucket."

Without missing a beat, I replied, "Colonel, I don't guess either of us'll ever get out of here. Your rank doesn't mean a damn. So I guess we'll just trade off."

Carmichael got a kick out of that and from then on we took turns walking in front.

Sometimes, as we journeyed into the neighborhoods, we'd come across villagers trying to survive in the ruins. As a group, they were in bad shape. Their clothes were in rags, they were living in the streets without adequate shelter, and they were clearly starving. If we came across a building that had survived the fire, or at least was partially standing, we had to knock on the door, and if someone answered, ask permission to empty their *benjo.* "*Benjo doozo kudasai?*"

For the most part, the villagers were like shadowy phantoms haunting a silent, dead world. Many were old. With their homes gone, families dead or separated, they had no place to go. The horizon showed no haven near enough to walk toward, and they spent their days squatting in a ditch alongside the road, seemingly lost, with no place to live and nothing to eat. They were clearly afraid of us, and one had to wonder what they had been through to be afraid of sick weak wretches such as us. But, they were much more afraid of our Japanese guards, who would beat a civilian as readily as a prisoner.

I never understood what motivated the guards' behavior. If they happened to spot a male civilian, there was a good chance that before the civilian could slink away, they would call to him, telling him to halt. As the guard approached the defenseless man, he would bark an order, bringing the civilian to rigid attention. Then, totally unprovoked, the guard would begin beating the civilian into the ground.

I never saw Watanabe beat a civilian, but of course they ran from him just the same.

The children were another story. When the guards weren't near, the children would run up to us in groups, staying just out of reach, shouting taunts at us like kids do. I never understood all the insults that they hurled at us, although I did recognize *B-Nijukyu* which indicated that they knew we were from B-29s. The kids didn't irritate me, though. They were just normal kids, surprisingly clean and healthy-looking considering their surroundings, and they had every right not to like us.

I was unable to hate the civilian Japanese that we saw from our garden details. These were not the murderous mob who had tried to kill me in Yawata. They were grandparents and children, trying to survive after their world had been burned to the ground around them.

One would have thought that as the gardens grew, some of the food might go to feeding prisoners, but such was not the case. We raised daikon mostly, so for me this wasn't a huge problem. I figured we weren't missing much. We continued to scrape for whatever bits of food we could find.

Our stomachs were always knotted with hunger, and while there wasn't a midday meal for us, our guard would let us build a fire to heat water out in the garden. The guard would spend the cold days sitting by the fire having his *ocha*, tea. While the tea would have been wonderful, there was still something gratifying about having a cup of *oyu* (pronounced *o-you*), hot water, when it was cold outside. It warmed us up and temporarily relaxed my stomach from its constant clenching.

I had learned months earlier that cold water was painful to a starving stomach. It just sat in my belly and ached like an iron fist in my gut. This hot water was a much-appreciated luxury. I didn't even think about what it would be like to have tea.

In addition to the hot water, we could occasionally come up

with a little extra nourishment while on work detail. There was a beach at the edge of camp, and sometimes the guards would send us down to dig clams and mussels for their dinner. We each kept a little piece of steel, scavenged from the town ruins, in a pocket just for this duty. If the guards weren't paying too much attention, it was possible to pry a clam or mussel open and quickly pop the insides into our mouths without being caught. While live raw clams might not be someone's first choice, they were clean and whole-some. There was such a feeling of gratification in opening wide and feeling that clam slip in.

Another special treat was palm hearts. There were several palm trees growing in the area. If the guard was out of sight and known to be occupied, someone could shinny up the palm tree, cut out the heart with another scavenged piece of metal, and throw the heart down. Several people could feast on a single palm heart, and as bland and woody as it was, it felt good to be eating it.

There was one feast that didn't get shared. During our daily march to and from the gardens, we walked along a shallow water-filled ditch beside the roadway. At one time or other, we had all noticed a large goldfish that had somehow ended up in the ditch. It must have been eight or ten inches long. I had my eye on the fish for weeks, maybe months, and spent many waking hours wonder-ing how to arrange for a chance to catch that fish for a tasty meal. At some level, I think I considered it my own personal property. I had invested enough time thinking about it, that it should have been.

Had I been more aware, I would have realized that every hun-gry man who marched in that column beside the ditch had to have developed the same attachment to that fish, for every pair of eyes turned to the ditch as we approached it and tracked on the goldfish until forced to turn forward again in the column.

One day on the way back to the barracks, I looked in the ditch as always and, to my dismay, saw that the fish was gone. With a feeling nearing panic, I wondered what could have happened to it. Some of the other men were clearly agitated, too. During the entire march back to the barracks, the loss of that fish was all I could think about.

When we reached the barracks, all hell broke loose. Everyone wanted to know where that fish had gone. Two of the guys, Smith and Lodivicci, almost acting as though the situation were funny, finally confessed to having doubled back to the ditch when the guard was occupied, and caught the fish. The nerve! How undemocratic! To make matters worse, they had even managed to cook it over our *oyu* fire before they ate it. They said it was the most marvelous thing they'd ever tasted.

My disgust knew no bounds. It seemed we could have at least had a meeting about that fish before one or two people took it upon themselves to catch it and eat it all.

They said it was only about two bites worth apiece, but this didn't quell my indignation. "Everyone in this barracks should have had the opportunity to have a little," I affirmed.

How could they have eaten that fish without me? I finally swallowed my anger, but it sat in my gut like icy water.

While most of our food procurement was done out of sight of the guards, there was one time when the temptation was just too great. One of the men, whom we called Snuffy Smith, was marching to the gardens in the column when he happened to glance down to the side of the road and see a handful of beans some villager had presumably spilled. Without breaking stride, he reached down and scooped up some of the beans and tried to put them in his pocket. As Snuffy's bad luck would have it, Horseface caught him in the act and lit into him, rifle butt flying.

The column came to a helpless standstill as Horseface repeatedly smashed his rifle butt into Snuffy's head and body. Snuffy was down a long time before Horseface finally spent his fury and stopped smashing and kicking him. I was certain that Snuffy had to be dead or near death. Horseface had beaten him into nothing.

Breathing heavily, Horseface signaled that we were to help Snuffy to his feet and continue our march to the garden. Several men stepped forward and managed to get the mangled Snuffy, dripping blood from head, nose, and mouth, upright enough to continue.

When we got out to the garden, Horseface lined us up and racked us to attention. Still visibly upset, he shouted, "Why he quick take it off?" As he yelled, he mimed Snuffy's scooping action of picking up the beans. "Why he quick take it off?" he demanded.

Horseface was angry that Snuffy had stolen the beans.

Someone in the column spoke up. "He wasn't stealing. Those beans were just lying there. Someone had obviously dropped them."

Horseface launched into a long, broken explanation. In Japan, he explained, if someone dropped something, even a handful of beans, whatever he dropped or lost was still his property. It was not for someone else to take. The person who lost those beans might come back and look for them. They should have been left there. Even if the beans sat there and rotted, they were someone else's property. It was wrong to take the beans.

Again, someone in the column spoke up and explained to Horseface that in our culture we also believe that stealing is wrong, but in our culture, taking the beans would not be stealing. And then he said something that Horseface had to have known. "We're hungry," he said.

For a moment, all the air went out of the much-hated Horseface. Using his boot, he smoothed a large area of dirt. Then, with the point of his bayonet, he drew a map of Japan and the eastern edge of Asia in the dirt.

"*Ima, Korea*," he said, pointing to where Korea would be on his map.

"*Ima, Nehong,*" he said, indicating the Japanese islands.

Then, pointing to the sea off Korea, he said, "*Takusan, kaigun,*" meaning a whole lot of ships.

"*Sekana, meshi,*" fish and rice, "*takusan,*" meaning a whole lot of it.

Then, looking up at us, he said, "Butta, cheese, too."

Then he drew a line where these ships were going south from Korea down the Shimenseki Straits, saying, "*Tokyo, ichi nichi.*" The ships were one day from Tokyo. "*Takusan, B-Nijukyu,*" a lot of B-29s. "Look. See."

"*Bokadon!*" he shouted. The B-29s bombed the ships. "*Taigun. Hiddish!*" The ships were finished.

And then, holding his stomach, he said, "Me hungry, too."

The End Approaches

"…and the rocket's red glare,
the bombs bursting in air,
gave proof through the night
that our flag was still there."

Francis Scott Key
The Star-Spangled Banner

By summer of 1945, it was clear to those of us in Japan that something would have to happen soon. Despite the food growing in the garden, we were getting less to eat. I was growing steadily weaker, and wondered how much longer I could last. Even the guards were hungry. If the military was on short rations, the civilian population had to be starving.

The B-29 incendiary bombing raids over Tokyo continued and we wondered how there could be anything worth bombing still standing in the city. We knew from the B-29 prisoners who were shot down more recently that nearly every city of any size throughout Japan was being reduced to ash. The Navy had a strangling blockade in place. No supplies were moving in or out of the country. How could the Japanese continue?

While the signs of Japan's defeat were clear even to us, the possibility of the war ending gave us only the smallest flicker of new hope. We were still in Japan, under Japanese control, and our captors hated us bitterly. It seemed a clear possibility that if the Allies invaded or if Japan surrendered, we'd be executed immediately. Besides, there was no telling when that might happen. We could easily be dead of illness and starvation before that time came. Or we could be bombed into oblivion by our own planes.

Because our camp was not marked as a POW camp, we could only hope that our little island didn't look too tempting to anyone who might select it as a target. There was no cover for us. We prisoners were locked in our barracks during air raids. All we could do was sit and listen to the deep vibrating drone of the big planes as they passed overhead, waiting to hear if the whistle of approaching bombs would follow.

There were some personnel changes at Omori during this time. While Watanabe and Horseface stayed on, some new guards were brought in, most of them mean. I remember one new guard who walked up to me as I stood in the barracks once, and standing close, he looked into my face, a deadly cold expression in his eyes, and said in perfect English, "How would you like a damn good American hamburger about now?" I didn't know what to do. I was sure this guy was looking for an excuse to pummel me. He didn't smile. He wasn't taunting. He was just cold and dangerous. Not knowing what to do, I just looked back at him. I didn't move. I didn't take my eyes off him. I didn't smile or speak or react. I just looked back at him. After many long seconds, our eyes locked, he grunted and turned away.

There was never a time to feel safe. Even though the beatings at Omori weren't a daily occurrence, we all jumped at the appearance of a guard, knowing that we could be beaten to death at the drop of a hat.

One sunny day, half a dozen guards came into the barracks and asked for volunteers for a work party. Fifteen or twenty of us warily stepped forward. We were ordered into line and marched across the footbridge. At the end of the bridge waited three beat-up open trucks. I was torn between my distrust of any new situation and eagerness at the thought of getting to leave the camp.

At the prompting of the guards, we piled into the trucks, sitting on the uncomfortable wooden rack beds.

We soon passed through the familiar burned village of Omori and headed out across the vast gray wasteland that was once a city teeming with people. The landscape was one of ash and the charred trunks of trees. The old trucks were slow and they coughed their way through the streets. It was impossible not to sobered by what we saw. The scale of the devastation was almost beyond comprehension. "What is the Japanese government thinking?" I wondered. Some of the B-29 crews in the barracks had participated in fire raids before being shot down. I knew that most of the other cities in Japan, large and small, were also burned to the ground. Their civilian losses had to be enormous. "How could they sustain this much damage all over Japan and not surrender?" I wondered. "And where did the survivors go? Why wasn't the population demanding an end to this?"

Yet, it was also exhilarating to realize how extensive the damage was. We were bombing them into oblivion just as I'd wished so many times. The evidence was in front of me. We were killing them, pounding them. I relished their annihilation. Surely it would all have to end soon.

But as always, that thought brought with it the other unwelcome emotion. "Yes, the war might finally end," I mused. We were winning, but I had serious doubts as to whether any of us in those trucks would be alive when it was all over.

The trucks drove on. We passed pockets of neighborhoods that had been untouched by fire. Usually it was just a single flat-roofed concrete building left standing, but sometimes a block or two had escaped the conflagration thanks to a fire break. These areas were inhabited, but we saw few civilians. The wooden civilian housing was gone.

After a couple of hours, the frequency of standing structures began to increase. We entered an area where there were even a few wooden houses left amid the concrete survivors. Soon the truck pulled to a stop in front of a warehouse. The guards motioned for us to get out. We were marched out to a patch of ground and given shovels, a few instructions, and told to start digging.

We were to dig an air raid shelter. It was grueling labor for a small crew of starved, sick men, but we knew we had to keep at it until it was done. Kennard was with us. He could only shovel with one arm, his injured arm now useless. We knew it would take days and we set to work.

We began by digging a tunnel. The dirt was thrown onto large straw mats which were attached to a pole and hoisted onto the shoulders of two men, much as we carried the honey buckets back at Omori. The dirt was mounded up in a designated area which would eventually become the top of the shelter, the mounded dirt making the shelter effectively deeper by several feet.

The tunnel wasn't large. You had to bend down a little to use it, and it descended about ten feet. When the tunnel was done, we began hollowing out a large underground cavern. In the end, it was probably forty feet long and six feet wide, all raw excavated dirt. The ceiling was six feet high, and some of us could stand comfortably inside, others had to duck. The guards brought in no additional light, and we had to dig by the light that came through the tunnel opening. We were like moles, toiling away day after day in our cave.

It surprised me that we dug with no supports or beams. While I was a little nervous being in the shelter, thinking it could cave in at any time, I wondered how effective it could have been during an air raid. It seemed to me that the concussion of a bomb dropping in the vicinity could easily cause it to collapse. A direct hit would go right through the dirt top. It looked like a death trap to me. I decided that the shelter was probably not intended to protect the inhabitants from the bombs themselves, but to give them somewhere to go in case of a fire raid. I'd seen a firestorm first hand and knew that if there was no place to run, a shelter such as this would be welcome and would probably save many lives.

Instead of trucking us back and forth to Omori, the guards had us camp at the warehouse near the shelter. Each night, we'd spread our thick bug-infested mats on the cold floor of the warehouse. The building was unheated, and of course we had no blankets. The days were warm outside the cool dirt shelter, but the nights were uncomfortably cold. Our meager food was brought to us in buckets morning and night as back at camp. I don't know where they cooked it. During the day there were buckets of water for us to drink from at the work site.

Work at the warehouse continued on as though we weren't there. It was a food warehouse, and civilians worked there around the clock moving huge bags of raw rice.

One night, there was a group of Japanese huddled together in the warehouse, arguing heatedly. There was a man with an abacus, throwing the beads around with blinding speed, agitated. I never knew what the argument was about, or what the outcome was, but tempers were boiling, and I guessed it had to do with money. Suddenly, a uniformed soldier grabbed one of the civilians, and while every one else stood and watched, started beating him. Of all the beatings I had watched and experienced in Japan, this was the most brutal. I thought the guard would never stop, he just pounded and pounded, punctuating his rifle blows with kicks, and pulling the man by the hair and throwing him against the wall. The man was soon unconscious and bleeding profusely, but still the punishment continued. We had no way of knowing, but I felt it would be a miracle if the man wasn't dead.

The day we completed the air raid shelter, they loaded us

back onto trucks and returned us to Omori. We returned to our routine of work in the gardens as though we had never been gone.

Even after we left the warehouse, the memory of the civilian beating bothered me. I was stunned by the ferocity of it. By this time I had seen several civilians beaten by soldiers. What could it mean? Was there no law in Japan? Was this viciousness a thread that ran throughout Japanese society, or was it a characteristic specific to the military? And if it was only the military, why?

When I saw the broken elderly men and women who huddled in the ashes of Omori, I didn't hate them. Nor did I hate the innocent children who taunted us. I didn't hate Watanabe, our good guard. But I had to conclude that, in general, the Japanese were barbarians. I knew, of course, of their aggression in the Pacific and the horror stories coming out of China. When I added to that my own personal experiences and observations, and those of other prisoners, it would have been difficult to draw any other conclusion.

To me, Japan was an evil place and the Japanese were as evil as the American war propaganda had portrayed them. Because of them, tens of thousands of lives were wasted. Their inhumane treatment of their fellow man appalled me. Had they no regard for human life? I despised them for their manure-covered daikon and their smelly *benjo* boxes. And I hated them most because they were probably going to rob me and my young friends of our lives.

Liberation

"But this island we're on floats in a new sea;
the doom in the guns won't ever be the same.
Strange things do happen. Maybe this is the day."

William Stafford
Waking Up in Bremerton

Something was up. The guards had been acting strange for two or three days. There was an intensity and agitation about them that was somehow mixed with something subdued, almost wary. Any change in the guards' behavior was a red flag, of course, but it seemed that they were suddenly less threatening than usual. They weren't as pushy. Could the war be ending?

The guards said or did nothing to indicate that this was the case, but there was definitely something in the air. Something big was happening somewhere. While a part of me rejoiced in the hope that the war might be ending, I also felt that we were in an extremely precarious position. I had always believed that if the Japanese lost the war, it was likely that they would just walk into the barracks one day and shoot us all.

Then, about the third day of this charged atmosphere, we were marched out of the barracks and assembled in the yard at attention. The camp commander was standing, waiting for us. He began a long speech in English. Nothing he said for the first several minutes told us what was going on. Then, he said something puzzling. Without telling us exactly what had occurred, he said, "Your country is guilty of inhuman warfare—a crime we cannot forgive."

I wondered what could have happened. What could have been worse than the incendiary raids? Was he talking about those?

He continued, biting out the words. "It appears that we will have to surrender."

And then he said, slowly and deliberately, glaring at us, "If we have to wait a hundred years, we will retaliate."

We were dismissed. This was the news we'd been waiting for, yet we knew that we weren't out of the woods. There was no riotous celebration or display of joy. Such gestures could have provoked the rifle-bearing guards into opening fire. We filed back to our barracks, attended by the still-present guard, and looked into one another's faces, wide-eyed, and filled with wonder. And hope.

Not much happened for a couple of days after that, except that there were a few changes in the routine. We no longer worked and nobody was beaten by a guard. There were no more bombing raids, leaving the skies eerily quiet. We figured the two sides must be talking. We waited anxiously, hoping that nothing delayed the surrender.

While the guards were still present, they seemed less energetic about their duty. We started to take small freedoms. We talked more and gradually began mingling with the prisoners on the other side of the wall and walking more freely to the *benjo.*

While there had been reports that Omori was filling up with prisoners being brought in from all over Japan, I didn't see anyone but the people in our building. Our barracks was at the edge of the camp, near the latrine building. I'd never been free to walk through the rest of camp and had no idea of what was occurring there, nor was I inclined to wander over to look. It simply didn't matter to me.

The guards stepped back farther. They stayed at the camp, but had little to do with us. We were free to move around more. An air of cautious anticipation pervaded the camp. We might be out of here soon. Many, including me, stayed in the barracks. I was too sick and weak to be curious or adventuresome. I wanted to hang tight, lie low, and ride things out.

Someone found some paint or lime and climbed onto the roofs of some of the barracks, marking "POW" in large white letters. "Boyington Here" was painted on ours. We wanted to be found quickly. We wanted out of there. Also, in case more air raids followed, we wanted our camp marked.

Aerial shot of the Omori prisoner of war camp after the prisoners marked the rooftops of the barracks.

We were living through frightening times. The now distant guards spent their days and nights fighting and drinking. The loud arguments in the guard house were continual. From the bits and pieces of rumor and assumption, we felt that the most fanatic guards were debating whether to ignore the emperor's command to surrender. More ominous, we were certain they wanted to kill the prisoners. We didn't know it then, but there were American prisoners in other camps who were quietly murdered in those final days. In one prison, twelve American airmen were marched out to the woods, where they dug their own graves and were then beheaded. Thankfully, there were Japanese at Omori to argue against such measures as heatedly as the fanatics argued for them. No doubt, Watanabe was in the midst of the fray, perhaps at great personal risk. I wondered if we had him to thank for our lives.

Then, one day, we heard that an American minesweeper had been spotted in the harbor. It seemed impossible! There were Americans, free Americans, that close! A few days later, the United States 3rd Fleet steamed into view. Before long, there was a line of battleships anchored in the Tokyo Bay, surrounded by hundreds of American vessels of every conceivable size and shape. The bay was jampacked. The air, too, had come alive. It buzzed with Navy planes. They flew over our island and we spilled out of the barracks, waving. The planes waggled their wings. They saw us! They knew we were here!

Hope grew inside me, although still hesitantly. It was beginning to seem possible. We might go home! Time in the barracks ground on nervously.

Soon, the Navy planes returned, flying low. When they got over the camp, they kicked out four-foot-square cartons of K-rations, which burst open as they hit the ground. The stronger men got to the boxes first and started passing food back to the weakest. There was no scramble or fighting as one might expect from starving men. Everyone waited patiently for his share.

The American food tasted so good. I remember the crackers, the joy of the salty crackers melting on my tongue, and the canned fruit, delicious peaches. I didn't have to eat it slowly, though, or chew each bit carefully. The food just kept coming, and we kept eating.

The Navy planes were followed a day or two later by B-29s flying over at 5000 feet. The B-29s were dropping barrels of supplies. The barrels were attached to parachutes and some drifted wide and out of the camp. Those that landed in camp came hurtling down around us. Some of the earlier boxes had crashed dangerously through the roofs of the flimsy barracks and we soon found it safer to stay in the yard where we could see things coming and dodge them.

Some of the barrels contained chocolate bars and cigarettes. While I didn't smoke, the taste of the chocolate bars melting on my tongue was unbelievable. It was hard to decide whether to eat them slowly for the taste, or to gobble them down quickly because there were as many as I could eat. No one could get his fill of food from the barrels and the crates. We just ate and ate. But there was plenty to go around, and the barrels just kept coming.

I loved watching those beautiful B-29s fly overhead. Each time they came over and waggled their wings, I was filled with pride. Those were our boys bringing us relief. Some of the crews might be my friends from the 468th. It was great to think about that.

Those food drops meant so much. One day I tucked away a part of one of the parachutes. I would take it home with me, with my rice cup and spoon.

The Japanese had disappeared. We had the camp to ourselves. While other men in our barracks might have explored the camp, I didn't. For me, this time before liberation meant only that I must wait. I had strength to eat and strength to wait.

Then, on August 29, a shout went up in the yard. A large white hospital ship was anchored just off the island and a landing craft was approaching. There was a dock outside the wall, and I later heard that Hap Halloran was so excited that he jumped into the water and started swimming toward the craft hundreds of yards away before he wised up and returned to shore.

As the armed Navy personnel walked toward camp from the beach, we pressed around them. Our liberators were so upbeat, so friendly, so healthy-looking. And clean! I was suddenly self-conscious and ashamed for them to see me so dirty, dressed in lice-ridden rags, but they had obviously been briefed not to react to our degradation. Their friendly smiling faces made it all seem okay. We were men again.

Silence fell as the commander of the landing craft slowly scanned the group. He saw the condition we were in and after a moment announced in a kind voice, "It's all over now."

The stronger men shouted and whooped. I didn't have the strength for such huge emotion, yet something inside of me released. I felt an inner sagging upon hearing his words, a realization of how sick I was, how easily I might have soon died at Omori. I stood on the beach, weak and dirty, and wept quietly.

Then our new commander announced that we were going to be evacuated to the hospital ship. The sickest were to be the first out. Friends from my barracks crowded around me and took me to the front. "Take him. Take him first," they said. Two sailors took me gently by the arms and walked me slowly to the landing craft. I turned to look back at my friends who stood on the beach watching as I walked away. "We're right behind you, Pick!" they called. I nodded and walked on.

As my feet touched the metal floor of the landing craft, I realized that I was finally safe. I began to truly believe, to feel that it was all over. Tears welled up again, tight behind my face. I didn't want to cry, not here, not now. I was going to live. I thought of my wife, Faye. I would see her again. I would touch her face and see her smile. Flashbacks snapped through my brain, Horseface, the Kempe Tai, Roberts' body. Mom.

I sobbed. They were taking me home.

The Journey

"Two vessels of his heart converged in wish
For the loud hour of peace: the bells, the pounding
Of the free blood again, the ears reopened
After such hush, after such lull of sounding."

Mark Van Doren
The Loud Hour

The landing craft filled up quickly and soon departed. We crashed and bounced through the waves of Tokyo harbor toward the looming white ship, the *Benevolence.* Omori grew small behind us.

The hospital ship was ready and waiting. A long steep stairway was suspended over the side of the ship down to the water line. I and others from the craft tried to climb up it, but none of us made it very far. We all had to return to the landing craft. Soon, a large platform was lowered to us, outfitted with hand rails and netting. Our escorts helped us, one by one, off the craft and onto the platform. Slowly, the platform started to rise up the side of the ship. The Navy men in the craft smiled, waved, and shouted, "Good luck!" then headed back to shore for another load.

When the platform reached the deck, there were sailors standing by to help us step on deck. "Welcome aboard. Welcome aboard the *Benevolence,*" they said. I was in a daze. Everything was so different, the change was so sudden. I was immediately taken below decks to a large shower room. The sailors were friendly and upbeat.

It helped me feel less self-conscious about how I must have looked and smelled. In a way, I was embarrassed to be there. I felt that being a prisoner of war marked me as a failure. I was relieved of my filthy clothes, which I'm sure were burned within minutes of my stepping out of them, and was allowed to stand under the warm, steamy shower for as long as I wanted. It would take several such showers before I would feel fully free of the grime that had been caked on my body for so long, but for the moment, it was enough to stand there, soapy from head to toe and warm.

I couldn't stand in the shower forever. I was too weak for one thing, but there were other things to think about. I wanted to get settled as soon as possible. I wanted to lie down, to start feeling better, to eat. When I got out of the shower, I was issued clean new Navy jeans, underwear, shirt and cap. It was such a luxury to dry off with a towel and step into those fresh, crisp clothes. I found myself in tears, then soaring with elation, and then back to tears. The smallest detail filled me with emotion.

I was assigned a bunk in the enlisted men's quarters. The bunks were clean and comfortable. And even though I was aware that there were probably some officers' quarters somewhere, I was so happy to be where I was that I probably never would have said anything. I was in no frame of mind to be picky about rank.

Four or five hours later, someone figured out I was an officer, and I was moved to an officers' ward. It had four or five hospital beds and Carmichael was in one of them! It was fun to be paired up with Carmichael again, especially considering that we were off the Honey Bucket Brigade.

The first day, though, all I really wanted was to eat and sleep. The doctors were great and our nurse, Lieutenant Bevans, was wonderful. She was of average height and weight, with dark brown hair. Her tour was nearly over and she was looking forward to heading home. She brought our meals to us on trays and I slept for hours. The clean fresh-smelling bed and pillows were so luxurious. My body sank into them and I didn't want to move. I welcomed the deep sleep.

Later, Admiral Nimitz and Admiral "Bull" Halsey came on board and toured the wards. They talked to each one of us and shook our hands. It was a big thrill for me, having these powerful men come welcome us and speak so kindly. I was overwhelmed.

At some point, late in the day, I was invited to go to the communications deck and call home. I got up and dressed and found my way to the busy room. I couldn't get through to Faye directly, but left a message with somebody to tell her that I was safe and on the hospital ship.

The evening of our liberation, they served us a huge dinner up on deck. There were over a hundred of us at the meal and everything was excellent. It was like something Carmichael, Newman, Mann, and I would have dreamed up in Kinoshu. They let us eat as much as we wanted that night, and most of us simply couldn't stop. We'd eat until we were full, run to the rail and throw up, and then come back and eat more. It might not have been the best thing for our bodies, but psychologically, it worked wonders. We weren't going to go hungry here.

Though we were free to move about the ship, I spent most of the time in bed the first couple of days. Nurse Bevins brought us wonderful meals. We had the best of everything: steaks, mashed potatoes and gravy, wonderful breads, everything I could dream of. I think for all of us, the temptation was to eat until we threw up and then eat again. I often woke up hungry in the middle of the night and made my way to the ship kitchen. It was staffed twenty-four hours a day, and the cooks willingly warmed leftovers for anyone who came in hungry. I was never alone in the dining hall. Regardless of the time, there were always two or three others having a meal with me.

At the time I arrived on board, I weighed in at 97 pounds. This was after gorging on K-rations and chocolate for several days. From that time forward, I gained two pounds a day until I leveled off at a bloated one-eighty. This was clearly unhealthy, but I couldn't imagine not eating if I had the opportunity.

The new small freedoms of liberation and the feeling of safety worked wonders. After a day or two, the ship moved from anchor into a dock. I was starting to feel stronger and I would often get dressed and walk around the ship for a few minutes to take in my surroundings. I even ventured down the gangplank and walked around the dock some. It was startling to me to be able to look around freely and safely. I reveled in being free.

The devastation from firebombing was evident even from the docks. Many of the nearby warehouses were destroyed and rubble filled the shipyard. I saw no Japanese during these forays off the ship. It was such a joyful feeling to be standing on Japanese soil, surrounded by victorious Americans.

On one such trip to the docks, I stumbled onto a beer party for the crew of the ship. I tucked a few cans of beer into my clothing and made a beeline for Carmichael's and my ward. We drank a couple of quarts each, feeling so special and clever for doing such a thing. It wasn't so much the beer that made us happy, but the freedom in being able to sit on our bunks and drink it if we wanted to. Life was good.

We had been on board the *Benevolence* for four or five days when Carmichael heard from an old buddy who was an aide to a general in the Army Air Corps. Two other generals had flown into Tokyo in the general's C-54 to pick up a B-29, wanting to fly it back and set a time record between Atsugi and Washington, D.C.. The C-54 was flying home empty, and Carmichael's buddy, the aide, offered Carmichael a ride. Carmichael jumped at the chance and asked if I could come along, too. And so it was set. We were flying home and would get there weeks ahead of most of the other prisoners. I couldn't believe my luck. What a special opportunity. I could hardly get it through my head that it was true. I sent Faye a telegram to have her and my parents pick me up at Letterman General Hospital in San Francisco. I'd waited so long, and now, in a matter of days, I would be home again, holding my wife in my arms.

The next morning Carmichael's friend and the flight crew picked us up in an American staff car and we drove through Tokyo to the airfield at Atsugi. We were astounded again by the miles of gray desolation. By now we had heard about the atomic bombs, of course. Carmichael's friend had shown us aerial photographs of the blast zone at Hiroshima and the huge barren circle where everything was simply gone. But as I looked at burned-out Tokyo, I couldn't understand how the Japanese had not surrendered long before. How could they have allowed this assault on their homeland to continue to such extremes without surrendering?

When we arrived at the airfield at Atsugi, I was again astounded by the devastation. Except for a temporary building the Americans had erected as an operations headquarters, there were no structures left at the field. It was just runways. Stacked in huge piles along the strip were the remains of hundreds of shot-up Japanese planes. There were wrecked planes everywhere, many clearly pushed off the runways just far enough to allow our planes to take off and land.

As I looked out over the airfield, I spotted the C-54. I nudged Carmichael and smiled. After checking in with Operations, we grabbed our barracks bags, which were filled with our Navy issue clothing, and headed to the plane. At the foot of the stairway, I looked around once more before stepping off Japanese soil. I would never come back to this awful place. As I turned and boarded the plane, I hoped I was turning my back on the entire experience. My life was ahead of me. It was time to get on with it.

The interior of the plane was a shock. I'd been in several military planes and not one could be called comfortable, with rivets and open beams sticking out everywhere. The inside of this C-54, however, was decked out like a private Pullman train car. There were two mess attendants to cook the meals and wait on us hand and foot. Food and drinks were served liberally.

The first leg of our journey took us to Midway, where we were met by another staff car and taken to the general's private residence. We stayed the night there, again not having to lift a finger to serve ourselves. From there we went to Hickham Field in Hawaii where we got the same royal treatment.

I was still wearing Navy fatigues, but they were getting tight on me. I was ballooning up at an alarming rate. If you poked me with a finger, anywhere on my body, it made a deep dent that took a long time to fill out again. I still had a way to go to get back to my normal weight, but I was a little concerned about the puffiness and was anxious to get checked out in San Francisco. I expected that the beriberi and dysentery would subside with time and more good food, and I was feeling stronger. The pampering treatment, thanks to the general, was certainly helping my recovery.

When we arrived at San Francisco, Carmichael and I both checked into Letterman General Hospital. We were issued new Army Air Corps uniforms. Because of the quick weight gain, we didn't look too bad. It was hard to believe the shape we had been in only a week before.

Still, the hospital bed was welcome, and I was happy to crawl into it and get some sleep. Carmichael's wife came, and after filling out some paperwork, he left. I was sitting up in bed when my parents and Faye showed up. They must have started out the day after they got my telegram, because they arrived in San Francisco before I expected them. They walked quietly into the ward, trying not to disturb the men in the row of beds. I turned my head when I heard someone moving nearby, and there they were.

My mother had tears in her eyes as she hugged me. "Oh, Ernest," she said, sniffling. My dad choked up and smiled. He was a large, broad-shouldered, barrel-chested man, six-foot-two and over two hundred pounds, who was uncomfortable showing emotion. He hugged me silently.

And there was Faye. She was still so pretty.

"Hi," we said quietly, smiling. She bent to hug me. I held her tight, not even sure that she was really there. It had been so long since I'd seen her. The images from the past year flashed through my eyes, more vivid, perhaps, than this new reality.

"How are you feeling?" she asked when I released her.

"I want to go home," I said. "Take me home."

Ernest and Faye Pickett in San Francisco after his release from the hospital. Due to the puffiness from rapid weight and water gain, Ernest's weight appears normal. Ernest's mother, Bernice, is behind and to the left.

Epilogue

Sept 6, 1945
The Secretary of War has asked me to inform you that your husband
1/Lt Pickett Ernest A returned to military control 29 Aug 45
                    Telegram from the War Department

I doubt that anyone who was a prisoner in Japan was ever able to fully leave the experience behind. For me, it has manifested itself in many ways. The first way is physical. I was only home for a couple of weeks before I had to be hospitalized again. I was having severe intestinal cramping that wouldn't ease up. Faye took me to the airbase hospital in Portland where it was determined that the inner lining of my intestines was sloughing off. I was diagnosed with chronic amebic dysentery and acute colitis. The pain was horrific, and I don't recall that they could do much for it.

I was transferred to Madigan Hospital in Tacoma, Washington, where I stayed for two or three months, after which I was on a strict diet of baby food for half a year or more. My recuperation at the hospital was slow, but as I gained strength and the pain subsided, I was able to participate in occupational therapy activities to pass the time. The war was technically over, but for many of the men I saw there, their injuries would be a part of their daily lives forever. I gradually recovered, but as I've aged, my intestinal problems have increased again, making me prone to serious flare-ups of Crohn's Disease and internal bleeding.

There is evidence that most prisoners of the Japanese ended

up with endemic heart disease, and certainly, heart disease has been another specter in my life. There was not much that could be done about my burns by the time I arrived home. The scars were angry and red. Even decades later, when they had paled to a white that would never tan, I always wore long sleeves and pants, even on the hottest days, not wanting to bare my hairless arms and legs. I was probably fifty before I overcame this so I could water ski with my children. Thankfully, the nerves and muscles in my hands healed and I was left with no long-term impairment there.

Psychologically, my POW experience changed me. The first years, I know, were hard for Faye. I was the same person who had left for Japan, but I wasn't as calm, I wasn't as loving and I had more of a temper. I was determined to put the experience behind me and move on with my life. I was unwilling to talk about it and threw myself into my new life, struggling to bury the past as quickly as possible and to go on as if nothing had happened. But the effects were still there.

I didn't want to try anything new or be in unfamiliar surroundings. When the POWs were invited to Florida for an all-expense paid R&R vacation, I had no interest in going. Faye would have loved to go, but I was adamant. No way. Although I had so wished I could go to college before the war, and the GI Bill now would have enabled me to pursue a forestry degree at Oregon State University, I couldn't bring myself to interrupt my work routine to embark on a new experience just a few miles away. I also didn't call the Chief Pilot at Delta who had suggested I call him for a job after the war—I, who had so loved to fly. While it still sounded like a wonderful job, and I even qualified for my commercial license after returning home, I never took the step of contacting him. It was too big a step.

Another effect of my experience in Japan was that I hated all Japanese. As much as I had enjoyed the Chinese people, if I saw an

Asian approaching on the street, I crossed to the other side or, if unable to avoid them, I spit on the sidewalk as they passed. I didn't stop to question if they were even of Japanese origin. I certainly didn't consider that they might be American. That they were Asian was enough for me.

While I don't believe that I had the drive for control that many ex-POWs report, it was many years before I comfortably sought out new experiences or wanted to travel. I also had a profound impatience for anyone who thought that in any way, "they had it tough." I was disgusted by anything that sounded like whining.

My wife stuck with me, though, and we built a nice life together. When I first got back to work after getting home, we bought a combination café/bus depot in Sweet Home, Oregon. We lived in a twenty-six foot trailer before buying our first little house for three thousand dollars. Later, I went into the logging and road construction business with my brother, Loyd. Faye and I stayed close to our families, worked hard, and after a few years, started our own family.

Eventually, my business desires changed and I had the opportunity to buy an auto parts store on the Oregon coast at Florence. Faye and I ran that business for more than twenty-five years. It provided a comfortable living for raising our three children and gave us a good retirement.

Our life in Florence was good. We were active in the community and attended almost every sporting event, concert, or other activity our two sons or daughter were involved in. Slowly, over time, my psychological wounds began to heal. For example, I eventually realized that I no longer hated the Japanese. There are a few individuals whom I probably will never be able to forgive. I hope they were hung after the war. But the generalized, racist feelings dissipated to the point where, when my sons, Dick and Tim, were in high school, I willingly hosted Japanese students on a wrestling exchange in my home. Their fathers might have been my enemy, but they weren't any longer, and these boys certainly had nothing to do with what had happened to me in their homeland.

I can't say I wish the Japanese nation well. It bothered me when we began importing so many Japanese cars into this country and I had to sell the parts for them, but that is more of a political issue for me now, not an issue of race.

My impatience and temper also cooled with time and my reluctance to travel or experience new things disappeared completely.

I didn't think about religion much in my early life. I believed there was a God and heaven, but spiritual issues were never on my mind, even in the worst moments in Japan. In the last half of my life, however, my views have changed, and my faith has become slowly, but increasingly, a large part of my life.

The close friendships I formed with my crew and with other men who were at Omori never faded. I have such respect and affection for them. Many of them are dead now, but I think almost all had happy lives. They were truly a group of exceptional men.

Carmichael stayed in the service and had a successful career. Although we didn't see each other as the years passed, our bond of affection was never broken. Dick Bishop, our senior gunner, was a steady and good man. He and his wonderful wife, Gerry, chose to live simply in the hills of Vermont. I always had tremendous respect for Dick and grieved when he died. Kazarian, too, stayed in touch. He was always a bright spot, so smiling and fun. He, too, has died after leading a full life and raising a family. Betty Roberts, the widow of my friend Bud who died our first night in Japan has remained our friend all of these years. She remarried after the war and lives in California. Humphrey, our fun-loving radar operator went home to Wisconsin, raised a family, and was a salesman. Our oldest sons were born on the same day. Our friendship has steadily grown over the years and we've seen one another many times at reunions and otherwise. He currently lives in Florida.

I saw Rewitz, our co-pilot only once after the war. Faye and I went to visit him in Washington state. He had always stayed to himself in the group, and didn't seem to want to pursue contact with us. Many POWs reacted this way, and I respected his wishes. We had always heard that Kennard, our excellent flight engineer, died a few years after the war. At least, we lost touch with him. We also lost contact with Shorty Armstrong.

Mann and Newman, who were in those dark cells with me at Kinoshu, have been consistent correspondents and friends, as has young Hap Halloran, whom I met at Omori. Hap became a successful executive with Freightliner and was instrumental in keeping the Omori B-29 survivors in touch. I don't think Hap has ever let more than two or three months pass without calling me. He's a generous, warm-hearted guy. He organized a reunion for the Omori group in Columbus, Ohio in 1992. It was a tremendous event.

Jim Pattillo remained in the service, reaching the rank of colonel before retiring and becoming a circuit court judge in California. Colonel Jim Edmundson reached the rank of Lt. General with three stars, worked at the Pentagon, and held several high-level positions during his thirty-six year career.

When I first returned home, I wrote letters to the families of the men who had died on my crew. There wasn't much I could tell them, but I thought they should hear from me. The uncertainty about Robins never left me until recently when, after fifty-five years of silence, I heard from Robins' wife. Her warm, caring letter eased much of the pain I had carried all those years, not knowing whether Robins had jumped. His body had been returned to her a few years after the war, so he couldn't have gone down with the plane. He had been ready to jump as I had thought. The haunting feeling of not knowing his fate and believing that his widow blamed and hated me, was finally released.

While my children were growing up, they often asked me about my war experiences. To them, it was some kind of ancient history. To me, the fifteen or twenty years which had passed were short. I downplayed much of the worst, but as they grew older, I eventually stopped avoiding the discussion. While these discussions were rare—after all it was not a topic that came up in day-to-day life—retelling the events no longer disturbed me. I think maintaining contact with the other men must have helped me handle much of what I otherwise would have left buried. Also, I wasn't the only POW in the family. My brother Maury had been shot down over Germany. While his captivity was drastically different from mine, it made our experiences a topic of discussion.

I have never been able to fully leave behind a feeling of shame about being a POW—that I failed at my job, that I let my crew and the nation down somehow—but I think the telling of my story now has helped resolve those feelings. Horrible things happen in war. I followed orders and they happened to me.

I've often thought of those four boys on my crew who died. They didn't get to raise families or have careers or enjoy many years of walking the Earth. They deserved to live to be old men as most of the rest of us have done. I will always miss them. The rest of the men on my crew went through hell in Japan, as I did. While the details of each story are different, the horror in each is the same. That these men did so well after the war makes me feel somehow proud of them. I am happy to know them all.

My feelings of patriotism for this country have not faded. I never question our need to have gone to war, and aside from that two-minute bomb run, I never question what our leaders asked of us.

The controversy over the dropping of the atomic bomb over Japan disturbs me greatly. I don't understand the mindset of those who wish to turn the Americans into the villains. The Japanese at that time were racist and imperialists. Their atrocities in China and elsewhere were well-documented before the Americans got involved. Before we dropped it, the atomic bomb was simply a new weapon, one which the U.S. hoped would make Japan reconsider their stance of fighting to the death. The numbers vary, but some reports estimate that the invasion of the Japanese homeland would have resulted in as many as a million U.S. casualties and more than a million Japanese. Without the bomb, that invasion was inevitable. The psychological effect of killing women, children, and old men who were set to fight to the death with nothing more than sharpened sticks would have scarred the hundreds of thousands of American survivors in unimaginable ways, not to mention the effect on the Japanese people who had already been traumatized so terribly by the war.

For me personally, of course, the atomic bomb meant survival. I couldn't have had many months left to live. Possibly, the onset of winter would have killed me. Had the invasion force arrived, all POWs would have been executed immediately. Standing orders found in Japan after the war confirm this. Yes, the atomic bomb was horrible. So were the fire-bombings. So was island combat. And so was the Japanese Rape of Nanking.

For years after the war, I was plagued by nightmares about my time in Japan. Now, fifty-five years after returning home, I still have a nightmare at least once a month. It is always the same dream, but there are two versions. I'm flying the Reddy Teddy when it explodes and catches on fire as it did on the mission. One version of the dream replays what happened. We bail out. I cry in this dream because I know that four of my friends are dying, and I cry for all that the rest of us will go through. In the other version, I somehow manage to fly the plane home safely. We are all happy and whole, laughing together. This dream is by far the worst, because after I've dreamed this version, I have to wake up and know the dream wasn't real, that reality was the nightmare.

Most nights, I sleep in peace. Those nights, I am free.

Faye and Ernest Pickett, 1991

Author's Note

K.P. Burke

There's a normal developmental stage in girls when they view their fathers as heroes. Following that, there is the difficult period when they learn that Dad is only human after all and they begin to separate from him. It's all part of growing up. I went through those stages with my Dad, too, but then something wonderful happened. I got to go back to the phase—only this time as an adult—when I recognized my father as a hero.

Dad and I began work on this story about ten years ago. For me, it was important that accounts such as this be recorded, because if humankind is going to continue to wage wars in this era of surgical strikes and live television feeds, we need to know what war really means. What happened to my father in Japan is not just a story of the past. It could happen again today. In fact, it is happening today in parts of the world most of us choose not to think about.

For Dad, I think the telling of the story was an opportunity for him to fully say what he experienced. Part of the camaraderie of former POWs must be that they have a shared experience that it is difficult for the rest of us to join into with understanding. But Dad wanted those close to him to understand and he wanted the world to know what happened in those dark cells in Tokyo. I think, for him, it was important that the sacrifices made by his friends and crew were not forgotten. The deaths of four of his crewmen bothered him always. He so wished they could have had the rich satisfying life he got to have. By his telling about them, they could live on somehow.

Writing this book with Dad was one of the most painful, profound, and joyful experiences of my life. Sitting across the kitchen table from him for hours over the years, I found myself in awe of this gentle man. He answered my difficult questions without flinching, dredging up details about events he could not have wanted to revisit. He was emotionally honest, at times bringing us both to tears. His memory, while susceptible to all the whims of recollection—better some days than others, variable on occasional details—continued to amaze me. In all but a few things, his accounts of events were consistent and sharp over the years of our work together. Sometimes I felt my most difficult task was in getting him to tell me about some of his accomplishments, things his modesty prevented him from relating until I prodded him, having discovered leads elsewhere.

Our process was simple. I asked questions, he answered, adding whatever came to his mind, whether directly related to the question or not. Our goal was simply to capture memory and detail. Never one to be dramatic, he was understated, telling me simply and stoically a story that left me staggering.

Dad repeatedly read everything I wrote or had me read it aloud to him, correcting my inaccuracies, adding information, or saying kindly, "Well, it wasn't quite like that," and then helping me to see a clearer picture. We did this so many times with every chapter that even if we have missed a detail, I believe we came as close to capturing the essence of his experience as we could. Apart from the final polish, Dad was involved in virtually every word of the manuscript.

He didn't get to see the finished book. Ernest Pickett died, peacefully, on September 7, 1999. It was a sunny day, and a warm breeze filtered through the curtain by his bed. He was cared for with attention and affection, his comfort of utmost importance to all concerned. He was eighty years old, filled with love for the world and for more people than he could count. I often think the reason he stayed with us for so long, despite his prolonged and difficult illnesses, was that he simply didn't want to leave everyone. He liked being here so much.

In his last years of poor physical health, he responded just the way some of his friends from Omori have reported he behaved there. No matter how weak he was or how much pain he felt, he was considerate, grateful, and optimistic. He told my mother that he loved her several times a day and thanked her for everything she did for him. She, too, is heroic.

I've discovered that our world is peopled with quiet heroes. Not all of them are veterans of wars. Some might be immigrants, or volunteers, or people who have overcome disadvantage. We pass them every day on the street and don't recognize them. Ernest Pickett was one of those heroes. In my eyes, he was a hero during the war, but even more, he was a hero after. He had every excuse to be less than he was. His challenges and faults were sometimes large. But to me, his heroism is that he continued to strive to become better, to love more, to give more, to have more grace for others. And he succeeded. When he had nothing else left physically, what was left was his love. That he gave freely.

Kristi Pickett Burke
May 15, 2001

Acknowledgements

K.P. Burke

A project can begin in a day with one burst of inspiration, but finishing it can require resources of time, talent, finances, and spirit beyond the reach of one individual. Such is the case with this project. I have many people to thank.

First, of course, I must thank Ernest Pickett, my father. To say those things for which I am grateful to him is beyond my reach as a writer. I don't know where to begin the list or how to end it. He knows. I know. My mother, Faye Pickett, deserves high praise in her own right. Dad and I weren't alone in this endeavor. Mom was a spirited participant in the entire process. She's the greatest.

My uncle and aunt, Gene and Edna Pickett, were among the first to say "go for it." They gave me the boost I needed when the project loomed its largest. Without them, it might have ended before it began. I thank Lt. General James Edmundson, "Colonel Jim," for writing the Foreword and treating me as someone special just because I was my dad's daughter. I thank Bob Humphrey, from the crew of the Reddy Teddy, for answering questions about his own difficult experiences and for providing details that enhanced the book. I owe many thanks to James Pattillo, who responded to this project with great enthusiasm, lending me volumes of helpful research materials and providing much-needed technical assistance. Any technical errors remaining in this book are mine alone.

I also want to acknowledge the staff at the Smithsonian Air and Space Museum reference and research area. Their passion for their mission is obvious. Their assistance during the afternoon I spent there is much appreciated. Likewise, I must thank the staff at the National Archives. I spent four days in various areas at the College Park facility in 1999. To a person, they were pleasant and untiring in their willingness to help. Something very right is happening at that facility. My hat goes off to them.

Many friends provided consistent encouragement to me, remaining always eager to see the finished product. Cathé Springer was steadfast and exuberant all along. She also got me a ride in a B-24 Liberator. It's something I'll never forget. I also want to thank Cynthia Whitcomb, not only for her professional feedback, her confidence-building, and her great suggestion for a title, but for all of those writing retreat days at the beach house. Dick, Tim, Mary, Ginny, Jean, Lois, Linda, Cherie, Leona, Sharon, Debbie, Janet, Nancy, Sage and Bruce all have made contributions in feedback or support. Space limitations prohibit me from detailing my gratitude to each, but I hope they all know how much they are appreciated.

My kids, Annie, Scotti, and Ezra put up with many mumbled "Hms and Ums" while I worked, and deserve thanks of their own. Annie and Scotti, especially, deserve much credit for being such self-reliant little tykes when I was "on a roll" in the earlier years of this project.

Finally, I want to thank my husband, Don, who made my dream his own and kept finding ways to carve writing time out of our lives. I am married to the kindest and wisest man I know.

Index

Pickett, Dick, 184–185
Pickett, Faye
  See Faye
Pickett, Gene, 1, 2, 4
Pickett, Loyd, 4, 184
Pickett, Maury, 4, 13, 187
Pickett, Tim, 184–185
Portland Air Base, 5, 182
pressurization, 20, 22, 25, 49
Preston, Robert, 38
primary school, 8–10
propaganda, 85, 92, 167
PT-19, 8

R

radar, 64–65
radar operator, 21
  See also Humphrey, Bob
radio operator, 21
  See also Kazarian, Chuck
Randolph Field, 6–8
Red Cross, 95, 125, 129–130
Reddy Teddy, 47, 48, 63
Reida, Al, (wife Sirrkka) 26–27, 28–31, 46, 61
Rewitz, Bill, 33, 44–45, 51, 76, 78, 84, 141, 145, 186
Roberts, Bud, (wife Betty) 32, 33, 46, 49, 76, 78, 81, 82, 83–84, 93–94, 146, 185
Robins, Hank, 32, 33, 41, 48, 49, 76, 84, 144, 186

S

Salina, Kansas, 25, 28–29, 33, 49
  See also Smokey Hill Air Field
San Antonio, Texas
  See Randolph Field
Savoie, Lt. Colonel, 79
self-arming bombs, 25
Skelley, Captain, 63, 73
Smith, Snuffy, 159–160
Smokey Hill Air Field, 25
South America, 49–53
square meal, 12
St. Johns, Oregon, 3–4, 5
St. Elmo's Fire, 64
Superfortress
  See B-29
superstition, 68–69
Sweet Home, Oregon, 3, 184

T

tail gunner, 21, 23–24
See also Nixon, Sam
telegram, 95
Tokyo Bay, 148, 149, 171
Tolzmann, Ray, 32, 44
torture, 91–92, 94, 103, 137, 146
transition school
See Davis Monthan Air Field
Tucson, Arizona
See Davis Monthan Air Field
two-minute bomb run, 76–77

V

V Mail, 129–130

W

Waco, Texas, 11, 14
Waldorf Astoria, 41
Watanabe, 147, 156, 163, 171
World Series, St. Louis, 31
Wright 3350 engine
See engines

Y

Yawata, 61, 76–77, 85, 87–89
Young, Tom, 82
Youngblood, 1st Lt., 13

Z

Zero, 24, 80, 82